"Anthony Bradley's analysis of black liberation theology is by far the best thing that I have read on the subject. Anthony's book is comprehensive and in-depth. He covers all of the bases, and thereby provides the reader with all of the information that he needs to understand the critical issues involved with black liberation theology. By covering such figures as James Cone, Cornell West, and Jeremiah Wright, we see all of the nuances involved with their approaches to the subject. His explanation of victimology, Marxism, and aberrant Christian doctrine make a noxious mix of ideas that would make any true Christian wary of anything even approaching black liberation theology. His keen insight into these ideas and his clarity of writing make this book a jewel. Anthony has done the Christian community a great service by writing this book. There was a significant need for a work of this type and its arrival is long overdue."

CRAIG VINCENT MITCHELL, Assistant Professor of Christian Ethics, Southwestern Baptist Theological Seminary

"I have read a number of books which purport to explain, define, or critique black liberation theology, but *Liberating Black Theology* is the easiest to understand. This is because Dr. Bradley unapologetically maintains a biblical, orthodox perspective while being sympathetic to the issues and concerns of black liberation theologians. The book should be required reading for any seminary class on biblical interpretation and for seminary students and pastors interested in understanding the history and struggles of the black church in America."

WY PLUMMER, African American Ministries Coordinator, Mission to North America, Presbyterian Church in America

"With irenic tone Bradley reveals the theological justification of racial separation inherent within the victimization philosophy of both first generation and second generation black theology. His analysis demonstrates how the vision of Cone and his intellectual offspring contributes to rather than resolves DuBois' problem of the twentieth (now twenty-first!) century."

ERIC C. REDMOND, Senior Pastor, Reformation Alive Bapt   neology, Was

3

LIBERATING BLACK THEOLOGY

Liberating
Black Theology

✝

The Bible and the
Black Experience in America

ANTHONY B. BRADLEY

CROSSWAY
WHEATON, ILLINOIS

ISBN-13: 978-1-4335-1147-9

ISBN-10: 1-4335-1147-9

PDF ISBN: 978-1-4335-1148-6

Mobipocket ISBN: 978-1-4335-1149-3

ePub ISBN: 978-1-4335-2355-7

Library of Congress Cataloging-in-Publication Data
Bradley, Anthony B., 1971–
Liberating Black theology : the Bible and the Black experience in
America / Anthony B. Bradley.
    p. cm.
    Includes bibliographical references.
    ISBN 1-4335-1147-9 (tpb) — ISBN 978-1-4335-1148-6
    1. Black theology. 2. African Americans—Religion. 3. Black power—
United States. 4. Liberation theology—United States. 5. Cone, James H.
6. Victims of crimes—United States. I. Title.
BT82.7.B725   2010
230.089'96073—dc22   2009026653

VP		19	18	17	16	15	14	13	12	11	10
14	13	12	11	10	9	8	7	6	5	4	3	2	1

To my parents,
Walter and Delores Bradley,
and to
Ben Hill United Methodist Church in Atlanta, Georgia,
where I first learned about black liberation theology.

Contents

Acknowledgments

I am deeply grateful and indebted to many people, without whose encouragement and aid this book never would have been completed: to Dr. K. Scott Oliphint and Dr. William Edgar for their patient long-suffering as they worked to shape my studies at Westminster Theological Seminary and make this project address critical issues; to Dr. Stuart Silvers, Professor of Philosophy at Clemson University who is solely responsible for flipping my brain's ignition switch; to the other three members of the "Fab 4," my fellow students Lane Tipton, Travis Campbell, and Flavien Pardigon; to my friends at the Institute for Human Studies at George Mason University for giving me timely categories to think critically about social ethics; to my friends and colleagues at the Acton Institute for the Study of Religion and Liberty, especially Rev. Robert Sirico, Kris Mauren, Jerry Zandstra, and Samuel Gregg, for providing funding and time to complete this project and for providing an unprecedented model of academic freedom; to friends and former colleagues at Covenant Theological Seminary, Dr. David Jones and Dr. Daniel Doriani, for providing me with initial and continued encouragement and support during my entire PhD program; to the Callejas family for providing me much needed breaks in Guatemala; to my editors Amy Ballor, Lauren Simpson, and Katie Moon without whose help this project would have been unreadable; to Adam Eitel and Jake Meador, my research assistants; to the amazing team at Crossway Books that helped to bring this project to life: Al Fisher, Justin Taylor, Jill Carter, and Ted Griffin; to my entire family for their tireless and consistent belief in me when others did not; and finally, to the triune God from whom all blessings flow.

Introduction

Before Sen. Barack Obama ran for president of the United States in 2008, most people in America, including those in the black church, had never heard of black liberation theology. Jeremiah Wright, Obama's former pastor of the Trinity United Church of Christ in Chicago, made international headlines when, in his support of Obama, he spoke about blacks suffering in America at the hands of "rich white people." Wright reminded us that Jesus was a poor black man who suffered under the oppression of rich, white people just as Barack had in his life. Wright was accused of being a racist for the seemingly racist comments made against whites and for black empowerment. Trinity UCC openly adopted a "Black Value System" written by the Manford Byrd Recognition Committee, chaired by the late Vallmer Jordan in 1981, which includes things like a commitment to the black community, the black family, a black work ethic, and so on. America was introduced to a church that said:

> We are a congregation which is Unashamedly Black and Unapologetically Christian. . . . Our roots in the Black religious experience and tradition are deep, lasting and permanent. We are an African people, and remain "true to our native land," the mother continent, the cradle of civilization. God has superintended our pilgrimage through the days of slavery, the days of segregation, and the long night of racism. It is God who gives us the strength and courage to continuously address injustice as a people, and as a congregation. We constantly affirm our trust in God through cultural expression of a Black worship service and ministries which address the Black Community.[1]

---

[1] See http://www.trinitychicago.org/index.php?option=com_content&task=view&id=12&Itemid=27.

When asked, Wright confessed that his teaching and the teaching of his church were nothing more than the views of a Christian tradition following black liberation theology, and in just a few months America became a black liberation nation.

I should probably write both Barack Obama and Jeremiah Wright a thank-you note because otherwise not many Americans would have been at all interested in black liberation theology, a focus of my research for the past decade, during the 2008 presidential campaign. When Wright's views became more public, it seemed as if I was on the radio every day, explaining to whites and blacks alike what black liberation theology is and what it means today. Glenn Beck asked me to write three articles for his newsletter and interviewed me on his radio program as well as on CNN *Headline News*. The black liberation nation was fully inaugurated.

This short book is meant to be introductory in nature. It's short but substantial. What is unique about this study is that it is interdisciplinary, engaging theology, sociology, anthropology, and economics. I use the term *black theology* to broadly encompass writings on Christianity in religious studies by a wide spectrum of black authors including theologians, authors of biblical studies, ethicists, and the like. This discussion will explain what black liberation theology is, recognizing that many nuances will be missing. I primarily focus on the role that victimology has played in the rise and fall of black liberation theology. I argue that the major flaw of black liberation theology is that it views people perpetually as victims. Thomas Sowell's and John McWhorter's works were hugely helpful for me on this point, and their voices echo throughout the book.

At the end, I suggest an alternate strategy for developing a redemptive-historical approach for understanding the black experience in America while remaining faithful to Scripture and orthodox Christianity. The thesis is that James Cone's presupposition of black consciousness construed as victim supplies a fundamentally flawed theological anthropology for later developments in black liberation theology, leading to the demise of black liberation theology. In other words, reducing black identity primarily to that of victim, albeit at times inadvertent, contributed to the decline of black liberation to obscurity (that is, until Barack Obama ran for president).

In the 1970s a Presbyterian theologian by the name of Cornelius Van Til predicted that black theology was eventually going to land flat and would not be helpful to blacks in the long run. As Alistair Kee now confirms in his book *The Rise and Demise of Black Theology*, that prediction came true. Kee argues that black liberation theology is dead. Black liberation theology was doomed from the beginning because its initial biblical and theological presuppositions were grounded in the reduction of the black experience in America to that of victim. Early in the development of black liberation theology, black theologians like J. Deotis Roberts clearly pointed out core weaknesses but, like most other critics, simply did not go deep enough to the presuppositional level.

Victimology also wove its way through the social ethics of black liberation theologians and set the stage for the adoption of Marxism as an ethical framework for black liberation theology after Cone. Furthermore, victimology set the stage for the development of black liberation theological hermeneutics by a rejection of "white" theological method for one that distinctively embraces the black experience, including the unique experience of black women articulated by womanist theologians.

This book suggests that for any black theology to serve the black church in the future, it must be formulated within biblically constrained presuppositions. Contextualizing the redemptive story in the black experience, then, can be done with the strictest fidelity to the will of God for human persons and creation, personally and structurally, as revealed in the Scriptures. Black theology has a future only if it presupposes the triune God and seeks to interpret the black experience through the lens of the whole of Scripture.

The outline of the book is simple. Chapter 1 gives a basic overview of the movement, offers some key terms, and gives a trailer as to where this study is headed theologically. Chapters 2 and 3 give a fairly detailed introduction to the work of James Cone, the chief architect of black liberation theology, and his theological emphases. Chapter 4 explores the role that victimology has played in opening up many black theologians to embrace a form of Marxism as the ethical framework for the black church. Chapter 5 details the story of why black theologians rejected traditional biblical interpretation on the grounds of Eurocentrism and offers a possible scheme that challenges the fact of white racism but remains faithful to the biblical text. Chapter 6 is the "now what?" chapter. In this book I offer an introduction to those who have critiqued Cone and others and offer what is essential for a Christian theology that is faithful to the text and also deals with personal and structural sin.

1

Setting the Stage: Defining Terms and Theological Distinctions

The fact that so many people are surprised to hear that anger in some of Reverend Wright's sermons simply reminds us of the old truism that the most segregated hour in American life occurs on Sunday morning.[1]

BARACK OBAMA

This book explores the identification of the human person primarily as a victim in black liberation theology, beginning with the work of James Cone, and suggests an alternate strategy for developing a Christian approach for understanding the black experience in America while remaining faithful to Scripture and orthodox theology. The overall thesis is that Cone's starting point for black identity as victim supplies a fundamentally flawed theological anthropology for later developments in black liberation theology. The flawed anthropology set the stage for the demise of black liberation theology beyond major recent criticism.[2] To explore the scope of this claim we must fully be introduced to the work of James Cone, the chief architect of black liberation theology.

---

[1]"Obama's Church Takes On Wright Controversy," Associated Press, March 23, 2008, MSNBC online, http://www.msnbc.msn.com/id/23771205/.

[2]Alistair Kee, *The Rise and Demise of Black Theology* (Aldershot, UK: Ashgate Publishing Limited, 2006). Kee argues that black theology is dead because black theology presents inadequate analyses of race and gender and no account at all of class (economic) oppression. Black theology simply repeats the mantras of the 1970s. While content with American capitalism, it fails to address the true source of the impoverishment of black Americans. Content with romantic connections to Africa, this "African-American" movement fails to defend contemporary Africa against what Kee believes is predatory American global ambitions.

WHAT IS BLACK THEOLOGY?

A clear definition of black theology was first given formulation in 1969 by the National Committee of Black Church Men:

> Black theology is a theology of black liberation. It seeks to plumb the black condition in the light of God's revelation in Jesus Christ, so that the black community can see that the gospel is commensurate with the achievements of black humanity. Black theology is a theology of "blackness." It is the affirmation of black humanity that emancipates black people from white racism, thus providing authentic freedom for both white and black people. It affirms the humanity of white people in that it says "No" to the encroachment of white oppression.[3]

The context of the statement may explain, in part, the intensity of the statement. This definition was forged at the height of the civil rights movement, when the black church began to focus its attention beyond helping blacks cope with national racial discrimination and move on to applying theology to address the unique issues facing blacks, particularly in urban areas. Bruce Fields explains that black theology seeks to make sense of the sociohistorical experience of blacks in the light of their confession that God has revealed himself in Jesus Christ.[4]

While black theology affirms blackness, that theology should not be construed as an antiwhite reactionary theology. The notion of blackness is not merely a reference to skin color but rather is a symbol of oppression that can be applied to all persons of color who have a history of oppression, as well as to other marginalized groups such as homosexuals.[5]

Black liberation theologians seek to apply theology in a manner that affirms the humanity of blacks in ways that they believe were previously denied. Saying no to being oppressive helps whites no

---

[3]James H. Cone and Gayraud S. Wilmore, eds., *Black Theology: A Documentary History, Volume I: 1966–1979* (Maryknoll, NY: Orbis Books, 1979), 101.

[4]Bruce Fields, *Introducing Black Theology: Three Crucial Questions for the Evangelical Church* (Grand Rapids, MI: Baker Academic, 2001), 13.

[5]Kelly Brown Douglas, "Homophobia and Heterosexism in the Black Church and Community," in *African American Religious Thought: An Anthology*, ed. Cornel West and Eddie S. Glaude Jr. (Louisville: Westminster John Knox Press, 2003), 999.

longer to see their oppression as normal and gives blacks an understanding that their lives matter to God.

Black theology begins with the life experience of oppression and formulates theology respectively. The overall emphasis of black liberation theology is the black struggle for liberation from various forms of white racism and oppression, and it views the imperatives of the Christian gospel to that end.

VICTIMOLOGY AND BLACK THEOLOGY

John McWhorter's articulation of victimology will be used in this study to denote a more robust understanding of the victimologist's way of thinking. McWhorter's description provides a critical context for comprehending the long-term effects of reducing the black experience to that of victim. In the end, victimology perpetuates a separatist and elitist platform that provides no opportunity for racial reconciliation.

Victimology is the adoption of victimhood as the core of one's identity.[6] It is a subconscious, culturally inherited affirmation that life for blacks in America has been in the past and will be in the future a life of being victimized by the oppression of whites. In today's terms, it is the conviction that, forty years after the Civil Rights Act, conditions for blacks have not substantially changed.[7] It is most clearly seen in race-related policy and through interpersonal evaluation among blacks. Ironically, notes McWhorter, the forced desegregation of the United States in the 1960s actually exacerbated victimology. During this time period, it became acceptable for blacks to confront whites with their frustration and resentment. This freedom of expression gained in the 1960s, coupled with a postcolonial inferiority complex, provides the historical basis for victimology.

McWhorter raises good concerns about grounding one's identity in the condition of being a victim despite abundant evidence to

---

[6]John McWhorter, *Losing the Race: Self-Sabotage in Black America* (New York: Perennial, 2001), 3.
[7]Ibid.

the contrary. The overall result, says McWhorter, is that "the remnants of discrimination hold an obsessive indignant fascination that allows only passing acknowledgment of any signs of progress."[8] Many blacks, infused with victimology, wield self-righteous indignation in the service of exposing the inadequacies of the "other" (e.g., white person) rather than finding a way forward. The perpetual belief in a racial identity born out of self-loathing and anxiety often leads to more time spent inventing reasons to cry racism than working toward changing social mores and often inhibits movement toward reconciliation and positive mobility.[9]

Focusing on one's victimhood often addresses a moral desire—it is a salve for insecurity. McWhorter maintains that many blacks are rarely able to see racial issues outside of the victimologist milieu and are trapped into reasoning racially in terms of the permanent subjugation of blacks by whites. He concludes that holding so tightly to the remnants of discrimination often creates more problems than it solves.

McWhorter goes on to explain that victimology often perpetuates racial tension. Blacks are encouraged by one another to "know your history."[10] The communicative function of said mantra is not aimed toward knowledge per se but toward remembering oppression and iniquity so it does not happen again. The irony of victimology is its tendency toward revisionist histories and creating an ethos that, a hundred years ago, would have precluded racial equality. Victimology, in other words, is *perpetuating* problems for black America, not solving them.

McWhorter articulates three main objections to victimology: (1) Victimology condones weakness in failure. It tacitly stamps approval on failure, lack of effort, and criminality.[11] Behaviors and patterns that are self-destructive are often approved of as cultural or are presented as unpreventable consequences from previous systemic patterns. (2) Victimology hampers progress because, from

---

[8]Ibid., 2.
[9]Ibid., 43–49.
[10]Ibid., 43.
[11]Ibid.

the outset, it focuses attention on obstacles. For example, in black theology the focus is on the impediment to black freedom because of the Goliath of white racism. (3) Victimology keeps racism alive because many whites are constantly painted as racist with no evidence provided. These charges may create a context for backlash and resentment, which may fuel attitudes in the white community not previously held or articulated.

Perhaps the most significant tragedy of a victimologist's approach, in McWhorter's view, is that it creates separatism.[12] Separatism is a suspension of moral judgment in the name of racial solidarity that is an integral part of being culturally black in America today.[13] The black experience is the starting point and the final authority for interpreting moral prescriptions, both personally and structurally. Separatist morality is not a deliberate strategy for accruing power; rather, it is a cultural thought—a tacit conviction that has imbued the culturally black psyche. Separatism is a direct result of victimology because whites are viewed in eternal opposition to the black experience; black America construes itself (albeit in many cases unintentionally) as a sovereign, cultural authority.

Separatism generates a restriction of cultural authority, a narrowing of intellectual inquiry, and the dilution of moral judgment. Mainstream American culture, when refracted through the lens of victimology, renders even the most ubiquitous cultural products and ideas "white." For example, Manning Marable, a professor at Columbia University, has explicitly exhorted black scholars to focus exclusively on "black issues." In doing so, he squelches intellectual curiosity (a basic good) outside the purview of the black American agenda.[14] Separatism is the sense that to be truly black, one must restrict his allegiance to black-oriented culture and assent to different rules of argumentation and morality. Few blacks, however, would admit that this is true. The truth, writes McWhorter, is that "the culturally black person is from birth

---

[12]Ibid., 50–81.
[13]Ibid., 68.
[14]Ibid., 52–53. Howard University is a historically black university in Washington, D.C.

subtly inculcated with the idea that the black person—*any* black person—is not to be judged cold, but considered in light of the acknowledgment that black people have suffered."[15] In the victimologist's worldview, black suffering is the proper lens through which all else is to be evaluated.

Ultimately, McWhorter warns against separatism. Separatism has, in the name of self-protection, encouraged generations of blacks to set low goals. Blacks have settled for less, not just in respect to racial integration, but also in respect to being human persons.

What James Cone and those who followed him came to develop is not only a theology predicated on the autonomous black person as a nearly permanent victim of white aggression but also a separatist theological system, all in the name of contextualization. This newly developed theology, based on victimology, not only jettisons orthodox Christianity but also impedes opportunities for ecclesial reconciliation.

DISTINCTIONS IN TRADITIONAL CHRISTIAN TEACHING

The natural question after being introduced to black liberation theology is to inquire about the major differences between this tradition and orthodox Christianity that would serve as the basis of critique. In other words, how does black liberation theology compare to what Christians have traditionally taught? In order to clearly delineate the objections that historic Christianity might raise against James Cone and other black liberation theologians, it is necessary to introduce a few key distinctions that demonstrate the dislocation of black theology from the rest of Christian orthodoxy. This section also will serve as a trailer of sorts to the comparative points throughout the book. As an example, I have chosen the theological presentations of Herman Bavinck and Louis Berkhof to summarize a general orthodox position on various themes in Christian theology.

---

[15]Ibid., 72.

The Doctrine of God and Scripture

God presents himself in the biblical story as the divine "I AM" (Ex. 3:14–15), the creator of heaven and earth and the great redeemer of his people. Orthodox Christianity has known God by his eternal love, power, and sovereignty as creator and redeemer. This God, as summarized by Louis Berkhof, is articulated in Scripture as a God who redeems. His attributes include his self-existence (Ps. 33:11; John 5:26), immutability (Num. 23:19; Heb. 6:17), infinity (1 Kings 8:27; Jer. 23:23), perfect knowledge (Ps. 139:1–16; Heb. 4:13), wisdom (Rom. 11:33; Col. 1:16), goodness (Ps. 36:6; Matt. 5:45), love (Rom. 15:9; 1 John), holiness (Ex. 15:11; Isa. 57:15), righteousness (Ps. 99:4; Rom. 1:32), veracity (Num. 23:19; 2 Tim. 3:13), sovereignty (Eph. 1:11; Rev. 4:11), and omnipotence (Gen. 18:14; Matt. 3:9; 26:53).[16]

What Cone and those who follow him fail to do is ground black theology in the full authority of the Scriptures. This fundamental presupposition regarding God and his Word is the only proper starting point for constructing any theological vision. As we will see in subsequent chapters, this is a central belief that many black liberation theologians jettison. If we do not begin with God in our understanding of the human person, we will not develop a proper understanding of what the human person is in the fullest possible sense.

Herman Bavinck provides a cogent understanding of this theological first principle.[17] Bavinck teaches that all knowledge of God comes to us from his revelation and that we, on our own, cannot appropriate its content except by sincere and childlike faith. Bavinck is quick to note that theology must be grounded in how God presents himself directly, not in the self-reference of the human person. If theology is not grounded in Scripture but is instead grounded in the mind of man, the entire edifice of theology, however skillfully and creatively constructed, collapses like a house of cards. No knowledge of God is possible except that which proceeds

---

[16]Louis Berkhof, *A Summary of Christian Doctrine* (Grand Rapids, MI: Eerdmans, 1934), 34–41.
[17]Herman Bavinck, *Reformed Dogmatics, Volume 1: Prolegomena*, trans. John Vriend, ed. John Bolt (Grand Rapids, MI: Baker Academic, 2003), 208–233.

not from human experience but from and by God (Matt. 11:27; 1 Cor. 2:10ff.). It is God's self-knowledge and self-consciousness that serves as our knowledge of him. Without the divine self-consciousness, there is no knowledge of God in his creatures. Bavinck continues:

> The knowledge of God in his creatures is only a weak likeness, a finite, limited sketch, of the absolute consciousness of God accommodated to the capacities of the human or creaturely consciousness. But however great that distance is, the source (*principium essendi*) of our knowledge of God is solely God himself, the God who reveals himself freely, self-consciously, and genuinely.[18]

The self-revelation and self-communication of God, argues Bavinck, is what makes theology even possible. The aim of theology, in contradistinction from a Conian approach, can be no other than that the rational creature know God and, knowing him, glorify him (Prov. 16:4; Rom. 11:36; 1 Cor. 8:6; Col. 3:17).[19]

What we will find in Conian and post-Conian black liberation theology, however, is that the goal of theology is to study the being of God in the world in light of the existential situation of an oppressed community, relating the forces of liberation to the essence of the gospel, which is Jesus Christ. The end is not the glory of God but the dignity of the black experience in America. This is a significant divergence from orthodox Christian theology.

The object of God's self-revelation, argues Bavinck, is to introduce his knowledge into human consciousness and through it set the stage for the glorification of God himself through the Spirit. Bavinck argues for three crucial foundations for theology: (1) God as the essential foundation, the source of theology, (2) the external cognitive foundation, which is the self-revelation of God as recorded in the Holy Scriptures, and (3) the internal principle of knowing, the illumination of human beings by God's Spirit.[20]

The following chapters present the consequences of discarding

---

[18]Ibid., 212.
[19]Ibid., 213.
[20]Ibid.

this approach and replacing it with a view of God and Scripture interpreted through the lens of the black experience. What Cone and those who followed him may not have realized is that orthodox theology was in no need of dismissal and that interpreting the black experience in America would take on not only a different vision but would also present ways of knowing God that are inconsistent with the biblical story.

The Doctrine of Sin and Human History

If the knowledge of God begins with God's self-revelation, then so do issues in anthropology. "When man fell it was [his] attempt to do without God in every respect. Man sought his ideals of truth, goodness and beauty somewhere beyond God, either directly within himself or in the universe about him."[21]

These conclusions are drawn from the theological articulation of biblical anthropology and from the pattern of the redemptive story found in Scripture. Herman Bavinck describes a shared dimension of human persons as sinful resulting from the Fall. The universality of sin is derived in Genesis 3 from the fall of the first human beings, which provides a nonracial common anthropology.[22] The consequences and punishments pronounced in Genesis 3:16ff. have direct bearing not only on Adam and Eve but also on their descendants and presuppose a communal guilt even in the present age. Because of the Fall, human history was forever changed and now becomes, says Bavinck, a history of sin, misery, and death. All human persons are now sinful by nature (Gen. 6:5; 8:21). In the New Testament, the universality of sin is explained beginning with Adam's disobedience (Rom. 5:12ff.; 1 Cor. 15:21ff.). Bavinck summarizes it this way:

(1) Upon the one trespass of Adam, God pronounced a judgment consisting in a guilty verdict and a death sentence; (2) that judgment was pronounced over all humans because, on some fashion that Paul does not further explain here but that can be surmised

---

[21]Cornelius Van Til, *The Defense of the Faith* (Phillipsburg, NJ: P&R, 1967), 15.
[22]Herman Bavinck, *Reformed Dogmatics, Volume 3: Sin and Salvation*, trans. John Vriend, ed. John Bolt (Grand Rapids, MI: Baker Academic, 2006), 83–85.

from the context, they are included in Adam; all were declared guilty and condemned to death in Adam; (3) in virtue of this antecedent judgment of God, all humans personally became sinners and all in fact die as well. God apprehends and regards, judges and condemns all humans in one [representative man], and also they all descend from him as sinners and are all subject to death.[23]

Regardless of our racial or ethnic backgrounds, we have a common solidarity in sin. Moral depravity, says Bavinck, is characteristic of all people by nature and does not merely arise later in life as a result of one's own misguided deeds. It must be remembered that humanity is not simply an aggregate of individuals but a dynamic and organic unity of one race—those made in the image of God (Gen. 1:26–27). As such, all the members of the human race can be a blessing or a curse to one another, and increasingly so to the degree that they themselves are more outstanding and occupy a more pivotal role in human associations.[24]

Jesus Christ is the remedy for sin. Bavinck maintains that when Christ descended to the earth, he became poor, though he was rich (2 Cor. 8:9); but when he rose and ascended to heaven, he took with him a treasure of merits that he had acquired by his obedience "to the point of death, even death on a cross" (Phil. 2:8).[25] Jesus Christ as Savior provides deliverance from sin and all its consequences and offers participation in supreme blessedness. The pinnacle of the benefits provided by Jesus' deliverance is reconciliation and atonement. Christ's sacrifice, notes Bavinck, has objective significance. In our solidarity in sin, God manifests his wrath against sins regardless of race, class, or any other distinctions among persons (Rom. 1:18; Gal. 3:10; Eph. 2:3). As sinners, we are God's enemies (Rom. 5:10; 11:28) and are in need of being reconciled to him through Jesus Christ alone. This reconciliation is not unilateral. "Not only must we be reconciled with God, but God, too must be reconciled with us in the sense that, by giving Christ as expiation (Rom. 3:25; Heb. 2:17; 1 John 2:2; 4:10), he puts his wrath upon him and estab-

---

[23]Ibid., 85.
[24]Ibid., 105.
[25]Ibid., 447.

lishes a relation of peace between himself and human beings (Rom. 5:9–10; 2 Cor. 5:18–19; Gal. 3:13)."[26]

The fact of the Fall and the accomplished redemptive work of Christ serve as the true foundation for the liberation of black people. The fruits of Christ's sacrifice are not restricted to any one group of people because of our common human solidarity as sinners. Bavinck describes three benefits that accrue from the reconciliation of God through Christ: "(1) juridical—that forgiveness of sins is our justification, mystical—consisting of the Christ being crucified, buried, raised, and being seated with Christ in heaven, ethical—through regeneration and being made alive, (2) moral—consisting in the imitation of Christ, economic—in the fulfillment of the Old Testament covenant and the inauguration of the new covenant, and (3) physical—in our victory over the world, death, hell, and Satan."[27]

The fact of sin, and the Fall then also, sheds light on the reality of structural or systemic sin. Within the context of America's short history, one need only look at the centuries of racial tension to discover that at times sinfulness has led entire institutions to organize to oppress blacks. This is not necessarily a result of the institutional structure as such—the church, for example—but is rather a result of the fact that structural sin is also a consequence of the Fall, as sinners assume positions of influence and power. Bavinck explains that for those in positions of authority and power, their own life and conduct decides the fortunes of their subordinates, elevates them and brings them to honor, or drags them down and pulls them along to destruction.[28]

Social injustice is rooted in a human history of sin. Structural sin must be evaluated on the same philosophical ground as personal sin because structures have actors (i.e., men and women) who have a shared solidarity in sin. The proper theological orientation on this issue will promote a proper ground for understanding, moving those structural problems toward the good.

---

[26]Ibid., 448.
[27]Ibid., 451.
[28]Ibid., 105.

ANTHROPOLOGY IN BLACK THEOLOGY AS DEPARTURE FROM TRADITIONAL ORTHODOXY

Nearly forty years after the first development of black liberation theology, the system has reached a dead end even with the light brought to this discipline by Jeremiah Wright. Black liberation theology is not the dominant theological platform in most black churches across America. How did this happen? One need only look to the leaders of the second generation of black liberation theology to discover just how far afield black liberation theology has ventured because many theologians denied orthodox starting points such as the final authority of Scripture, biblical definitions of sin and redemption, the doctrines of God and redemption by means of substitutionary atonement, and the like.

As we shall see in the chapters that follow, today's black theology, in the Conian tradition, has redefined key doctrines, some might argue, and thus nearly turned Christianity into a completely different form of Christianity. We see this, for example, in the anthropology of Cone's chief disciple, Dwight N. Hopkins, one of the most brilliant and prominent second-generation black liberation theologians in the world and a former student of James Cone who is now teaching at the University of Chicago Divinity School. Hopkins's views on anthropology, which provide a representative snapshot of the consequences of Cone's initial vision and trajectory, reveal the outcome of developing a theology that does not begin with God's condescended revealing of himself to human beings in nature as well as in the Scriptures (Rom. 1:18–32).

Hopkins, in contrast to the traditional orthodoxy outlined in this chapter, holds that the ultimate "presuppositions" for a Christian theological anthropology must be rooted in "culture, selves/self, and race."[29] Here reducing black identity to that of "victim" supplies a flawed theological anthropology that lives on in black liberation theology decades after Cone's initial works.

According to Hopkins, culture is the totality of human labor, a

---

[29]Dwight N. Hopkins, *Being Human: Race, Culture, and Religion* (Minneapolis: Fortress Press, 2005), 162–163.

fluid dynamic of mutual effectivity between material base and ideational superstructure.[30] Labor as a theological category sheds light on the dimensions of one's existence within particular cultures. A person's inner characteristics and ethical practices, adjudicated by community, determine the quality of one's aesthetic beauty within culture. Hopkins introduces the notion of a generic "spirit," which locates one's personal identity in the following way: "Healthy spirit, in contrast to demonic spirituality, is the creativity unfolding in culture and vivifies both human labor and the aesthetic."[31] Spirit, in Hopkins's vision, mediates a sense of service to those who are on the economic and social peripheries of the world with a sense of hyperindividualism.

The second presupposition in Hopkins's theological anthropology is the notion of selves and self. Selves and self craft culture out of human interaction. A priority for a community of selves is developed in relation to individual selves. Hopkins writes, "The idea of selves brings together communal values (that is, sharing, mutual aid, caring for others, interdependence, solidarity, reciprocal obligations, and social harmony), community (that is, interpersonal relations), and common good (that is, the end product or goal defined by what is materially and spiritually fitting for the collective selves and individual participants)."[32] In ongoing dialogue between individual selves, people can be liberated from personal psychological demons as well as from outside oppression. It is this construction that secures the uniqueness of the self.

The third starting point for Hopkins's theological anthropology is race.[33] Race "localized in the United States (though having global implications, given the hegemony of U.S. monopoly capitalist empire) means explicitly combining biological or God-given phenotype with malleable sociological characteristics."[34] Race, for

---

[30]Ibid., 164.
[31]Ibid.
[32]Ibid.
[33]William R. Jones, "Divine Racism: The Unacknowledged Threshold Issue for Black Theology," in *African American Religious Thought: An Anthology*, 854.
[34]Hopkins, *Being Human*, 165. Also see Vincent Harding, "The Religion of Black Power," in *African American Religious Thought: An Anthology*, 721–722.

Hopkins, is constantly reflective of the "white supremacist spiritual-ity" that is pervasive in theology today with only occasional excep-tions.[35] Since, according to Hopkins, the global human race evolved out of Africa, theological anthropology must develop through this "rational fact" because it underlines the "dangerous but spurious popular and scientific notions about Europe as the land of human origins."[36] White supremacy triumphed in the theological catego-ries, ideas, and imperatives during the seventeenth, eighteenth, and nineteenth centuries in Europe and North America. As such, this white supremacist tradition created the anthropological categories that led to oppression of Africans and their descendants in the West.

Beginning here, Hopkins holds that God has a special affinity for the African-American poor and affirms the positive cultural and political traditions and practices of this community.[37] In Hopkins's view, poor blacks remain perpetual victims. The contribution of the black poor to our understanding of culture, selves, and race provides an example of God's preference for the poor. Christianity remains a means for poor blacks to achieve upward social mobility and eco-nomic liberation. As such, the mission and work of the kingdom of God are reduced to meeting material, political, and social needs for poor and working-class blacks. The continuation of Marxist catego-ries, as will be explored later, provides a seamless adoption of the secular humanists' presuppositions without antithesis.[38]

Forty years after Cone's initial work, anthropology in black liberation theology recasts what it means to be human, not in rela-

---

[35]Victor Anderson, "Ontological Blackness in Theology," in *African American Religious Thought: An Anthology*, 897.

[36]Hopkins, *Being Human*, 164.

[37]Ibid. Also see Hans A. Baer and Merrill Singer, "Religious Diversification during the Era of Advanced Industrial Capitalism," in *African American Religious Thought: An Anthology*, 509.

[38]We do find, however, a movement to introduce socialism into the ethical framework of the black church as early as the end of the nineteenth century. The Rev. George Washington Woodbey was the leading Negro Socialist in the first decade of the twentieth century. In his 1904 defense of Marxism, Woodbey writes, "Marx, the greatest philosopher of modern times, belongs to the same wonderful Hebrew race that gave to the world Moses, the Law giver, the kings and prophets, and Christ the Son of the Highest, with his apostles, who, claim gave us the Bible that, we claim, teaches socialism. Doubtless Marx, like other young Hebrews, was made acquainted with the economic teachings of Moses, and all the rest of the Old Testament sages and prophets, whatever we find him believing in after life. If we are able to show that the Bible opposes both rent, interest, and profits, and the exploiting of the poor, then it stands just where the Socialists do." Quoted in Philip S. Foner, "Reverend George Washington Woodbey: Early Twentieth-Century California Black Socialist," in *African American Religious Thought: An Anthology*, 661.

tion to God, but in relation to social structures as the starting point. In this vision, two key presumptions remain: (1) all whites have methodically sought to dominate blacks, which has "produced and continues to replicate an increased impoverishment of black folk economically and politically," and (2) poor blacks are only poor because of structural, premeditated oppression.[39] The premeditated perpetual oppression is, in part, associated with the Leninist idea that the poor are poor because the wealthy take from them. White theological systems not only keep blacks oppressed but also provide them with a deficient theological system to understand their own experience in light of culture, the self, and race. Full humanity is not achieved as a consequence of union with Christ but rather through being a participant in the liberation of poor and working-class people caught in structures and conditions of oppression—i.e., solidarity with victims. Ethics is reconstituted in terms of issues exclusive to black communities.[40] When social arrangements are reordered by race and class (but primarily by class in the case of blacks), authentic liberation occurs. In order for liberation to happen, whites must redistribute wealth and intellectual property and raise the standard material prosperity of all peoples in order to attain true equality. Otherwise blacks will remain victims.

The second generation of black liberation theology adopts a fundamental anthropology that believes that "all human beings are created with a spiritual purpose (or transcendent or ultimate vision) to share in the material resources of the earth."[41] This sharing has special priority when considering people at the margins of society. The individual, then, only has meaning in service to others, especially in the redistribution of unearned wealth. What makes a person human is that he is involved in service to the most vulnerable in society. To further demonstrate this idea, Hopkins, like many second-generation black liberation theologians, appeals to black folktales, not the Bible, as the paradigm and authoritative proof texts for empowering poor

---

[39]Hopkins, *Being Human*, 167.
[40]See Cheryl J. Sanders, *Empowerment Ethics for a Liberated People: A Path to African American Social Transformation* (Minneapolis: Fortress Press, 1995).
[41]Hopkins, *Being Human*, 168.

blacks. Black folklore shapes his theological anthropology by utilizing the following four paradigms or genres:

> First, the black *trickster* type deploys the discourse of *reversal* as linguistic sign and as ethical play and reveals a spirituality of *human flourishing*. Second, the black *conjurer* figure works with *nature* to manipulate spiritual powers of *all creation* for human advancement. Third, the *outlaw* type commands an array of diffused *ambiguity*, with a spirituality of *individual desire*. Fourth, the *Christian witness* figure most consistently yields *empowerment* for the most vulnerable, thus a spirituality of *compassion for the poor*. All characters or archetypes display some dimensions of healthy theological anthropology—what God has created humans to be and what humans are called to become still today: individuality serving equal identities, shared spaces, and mutual ownership of wealth in community.[42]

Theology for Hopkins is the revelation of a spirit of liberation through Jesus Christ, yet "informed" by lessons from non-Christian expressions of this same spirit. As such, black folklore has an elevated authority to form and shape the applications and understandings of Christian theology. Hopkins believes that Jesus is neither the only nor the exclusive incarnation of the truth.[43] Theological anthropology is enhanced in the vision of black liberation by non-Christian expression of "how the spirit works" and evolves from comparing different versions of the four literary genres in black folk culture. It is Hopkins's hope that the future of theological anthropology will reject false distinctions between the sacred and the secular in order to develop a more rich vision for the Christian life by embracing the wisdom gathered from black folktales. It would be easy to charge some black theologians with a form of syncretism for mixing Christianity with black folk religiosity.

In Hopkins's quest on behalf of the marginalized for communal life in a world of capitalist restrictions, the four folk paradigms

---

[42]Ibid., 169, italics his. Cornel West also makes a case for a wealth redistribution model for the black church from a Marxist viewpoint in *Prophesy Deliverance!: An Afro-American Revolutionary Christianity* (Philadelphia: Westminster Press, 1982).

[43]Hopkins, *Being Human*, 170.

provide a normative characteristic of God. Black folktales explain how the four themes of reversal, nature, ambiguity, and empowerment embody the application of love and the spread of freedom in Hopkins's vision. The *imago Dei* (image of God) in the flesh "stands for human efforts to open space for those once changed internally by psychological sin and externally by structural sin."[44] Freedom in theological anthropology means that humans are to act as stewards with equal collective ownership of all wealth as demonstrated in the commands given for life in the Garden of Eden.

Traditional theological categories, originally established by whites, are redefined to harmonize with the agenda of economic upward mobility for victims and those at the margins. Hopkins continues, "The Fall—the rise of monopoly capitalism—gave birth to and marginalized the majority of the world's population in the modern period."[45] The biblical story after the Fall, then, is a drama about how to move the oppressed out of spiritual and material slavery, how to relocate individual and corporate sin into loving the poor and working people. Proper expressions of biblical love and care for creation, then, are found in collective ownership.

The four paradigms in black folktales provide an opportunity to put more flesh on the bones of what is missing in Scripture. The presupposition for building true community is cast in socioeconomic terms as equal access to the earth's resources, the assertion of self as the bearer of an ultimate vision for realization of one's potentiality, and equal status within human relationships for all people, regardless of race.[46]

Hopkins's views, of course, present many problems for the redemptive-historical approach. As stated earlier, black liberation theology holds to a set of presuppositions that contradict traditional orthodox views. Further, Hopkins's second-generation inauguration of a theological program based on the premise of victimology does not exist in a vacuum and has its own complicated historical theology, which is the focus of the remainder of the book.

---

[44]Ibid., 184. For a similar view on black theology, see Stephen G. Ray Jr., *Do No Harm: Social Sin and Christian Responsibility* (Minneapolis: Fortress Press, 2003).
[45]Hopkins, *Being Human*, 184.
[46]Ibid., 186.

CONCLUSION

Black theology originated as a reaction to the lack of attention paid to the plight of blacks by Protestants during the civil rights movement. When reading second-generation theologians like Hopkins for the first time, one is immediately prompted with the question, how did the second generation of black liberation theology come to maintain a victimologist approach, which ultimately led to its demise? Upon examination of the original theological positions, hermeneutics (methods of biblical interpretation), and ethics of black liberation theology, with victimology as the anthropological starting point, the dismal future of black liberation theology becomes clear beyond even what Alistair Kee suggests in his book *The Rise and Demise of Black Theology*. Issues of autonomy, the authority of the black experience, the role of Scripture, definitions of sin and redemption, and ultimately the doctrines of God and redemption each play key roles in the development of black theology.

In the next two chapters, the theology of James Cone will be examined in detail, as well as his departure from traditional Christian orthodox theology, which ultimately led the second generation astray. The second generation of black liberation theologians, which includes Hopkins and others, is simply perpetuating new, nontraditional positions that developed from the early works of first-generation black liberation theologians such as James Cone, Gayraud Wilmore, and Cornel West.

Because black liberation theology jettisoned the traditional distinctions of orthodoxy and chose a platform of autonomy, it was destined to become unhelpful to the black church at large and to the ever-changing realities of black life in America. Again, the question remains, how did this happen? The chapters that follow will define key themes and concepts generally rejected in the black liberation tradition and will subsequently employ them to evaluate theological developments from the time of Cone's initial presentation of black liberation theology in 1969.

2

America the Broken: Cone's Sociopolitical Ethical Context

In the late 1960s, when Dr. James Cone's powerful books burst onto the scene, the term "black liberation theology" began to be used. I do not in any way disagree with Dr. Cone, nor do I in any way diminish the inimitable and incomparable contributions that he has made and that he continues to make to the field of theology. Jim, incidentally, is a personal friend of mine.[1]

REV. JEREMIAH WRIGHT

The prophetic theology of the black church during the days of segregation, Jim Crow, lynching, and the separate-but-equal fantasy was a theology of liberation.[2]

REV. JEREMIAH WRIGHT

When the first images of Jeremiah Wright's seemingly angry preaching against whites was broadcast on Fox News, most Americans were wondering, *Why would he say such things about America? It seems so unchristian and unpatriotic.* To understand this, as one of my professors used to quip, "Context is our friend." This chapter will introduce in more detail some of the contextual issues that serve as the basis for the sorts of objections that liberationists like Jeremiah Wright and James Cone have against America, white people, and what is called "the white church."

---

[1] "Reverend Wright at the National Press Club," *New York Times* (April 28, 2008); http://www.nytimes.com/2008/04/28/us/politics/28text-wright.html?_r=2&pagewanted=2.
[2] Ibid.

In recent decades, the social gospel movement, liberation theology, and secular political theory have filled a void by addressing social issues left largely untouched by conservative Christian scholarship. James Cone developed black theology in the late 1960s out of a frustration that at no point in his seminary or PhD studies, at predominantly white schools, was there any discussion about racism and segregation in America. While completing a Bachelor of Divinity program at Garrett Biblical Institute (now Garrett-Evangelical Theological Seminary), his frustration turned into what may seem like bitter anger. His experience of encountering racism among United Methodists at Garrett, along with his professors' refusal to see "racism as a *theological* problem," prompted Cone to attempt to make these theological connections on his own.[3] For Cone, it seemed that despite studying during the height of the civil rights movement, the central problems being addressed in American theology were issues important only in the European context.

After completing his PhD at Northwestern University, Cone published *Black Theology and Black Power* in 1969 as an attempt to bring theology into close contact with the social issues blacks were experiencing in America in the late 1960s. Immediately after publication, the book launched a movement that continues to shape and form the theological positions of many seminaries around the world. The purpose of this chapter is to summarize the foundations of Cone's black liberation theology as a system and to introduce the theological trajectory fashioned by the first generation of black liberation theologians.

CONE'S THEOLOGICAL BACKGROUND

James Cone's early theological texts are highly dependent on the theology of Karl Barth. This is likely a result of his PhD dissertation, "The Doctrine of Man in the Theology of Karl Barth." In general, Cone's perspective, which can be easily placed within the twentieth-century liberal and neoorthodox Protestant traditions, is primarily

---

[3] James Cone, *My Soul Looks Back* (Maryknoll, NY: Orbis Books, 1986), 37, italics his.

derived from philosophers and theologians such as Immanuel Kant, Jean-Paul Sartre, Friedrich Schleiermacher, Albert Ritschl, Karl Barth, Paul Tillich, Rudolf Bultmann, Reinhold Niebuhr, Dietrich Bonhoeffer, Jürgen Moltmann, Wolfhart Pannenberg, and other neoorthodox theologians.

Cone, in seeking to develop something unique for the black experience, was eager to develop a theology that went beyond nineteenth-century liberalism and neo-orthodoxy and often clearly states his departure from each tradition at key points, dealing with issues specific to the black community. Cone, orienting much of his theology on the work of men such as Jean-Paul Sartre, works out the implications of his belief in the autonomy of black consciousness by stressing the fact that human existence precedes essence.

Other than a few book reviews, no detailed theological critique has been made of Cone's work from an evangelical perspective that addresses in an interdisciplinary fashion black theology at the time of his writing and in the years following his initial work. Such a critique will be the focus of the chapters to follow. The goal of this chapter is to consider Cone with as much charity and grace as possible because Cone's deepest desire was to help black people address the mystery of white oppression and racism that engulfed much of our world at the time of his early writings.

CONE'S THEOLOGICAL STARTING POINTS

James Cone, in his book *A Black Theology of Liberation*, develops black theology as a system, beginning by articulating liberation as the starting point and content of theology.[4] Many of these initial formulations serve as the background for later developments of black theology as a theological system.[5] According to Cone, Christian theology is a theology of liberation—*a rational study of the being of God in the world in light of the existential situation of an oppressed community, relating the forces of liberation to the*

---

[4]James Cone, *A Black Theology of Liberation* (Maryknoll, NY: Orbis Books, 1990).
[5]See James H. Evans Jr., *We Have Been Believers: An African-American Systematic Theology* (Minneapolis: Fortress Press, 1992).

essence of the gospel, which is Jesus Christ.[6] The authoritative existential situation described in the study of the being of God is correlated to the black experience in America. Black consciousness and the black experience of oppression orient Cone's system around the principle of the self-sufficient inwardness of the human consciousness in general and the black consciousness in particular—i.e., one of victimization from oppression.[7]

One of the tasks of black theology, says Cone, is to analyze the nature of the gospel of Jesus Christ in light of the experience of oppressed blacks. As such, they will see the gospel as inseparable from their humiliated condition, which bestows on them the necessary power to break the chains of oppression. For Cone, no theology is Christian theology unless it arises from oppressed communities and interprets Jesus' work as that of liberation. Christian theology is understood in terms of systemic and structural relationships between two main groups: victims (the oppressed) and victimizers (oppressors). In Cone's context, writing in the late 1960s and early 1970s, the great event of Christ's liberation was freeing African-Americans from the centuries-old tyranny of white racism and white oppression.

Cone grounds the liberation motif in the biblical story of redemption by noting that: (1) God chose Israel because they were being oppressed; (2) the rise of Old Testament prophecy is due primarily to the lack of social justice as God is revealed as the God of liberation for the oppressed; and (3) Jesus reaffirms the preeminence of God as liberator because Jesus locates his ministry among the poor and the oppressed (Luke 4:18–19).[8] Theology, then, is the study of God's liberating activity on behalf of those who are oppressed. Assisting the oppressed, in Cone's view, is the sole reason for the existence of theology as a discipline.

American "white theology," which Cone never clearly defines, is charged with having failed to help blacks in the struggle for lib-

---

[6]See Cone, *A Black Theology of Liberation*, 1.
[7]See Cornelius Van Til, *Black Theology and Black Power*, CD-ROM.
[8]Cone, *A Black Theology of Liberation*, 2–3.

eration. Black theology exists because "white religionists" failed to relate the gospel of Jesus to the pain of being black in a white racist society.[9] According to Cone, black theology is legitimate as a theological system primarily because it arose out of a concept of oppression, which is the predominant condition of God's people; and secondly, it is Christ-centered. Jesus, as ultimate liberator, is the only means of freeing blacks from white oppression.

Cone seeks to distinguish his system in contradistinction from "conservatives" because in the fight against evil there is no perfect guide, including the Bible, for discerning God's movement in the world. In the Conian system, the Bible is a "valuable symbol for pointing to God's revelation in Jesus, but it is not self-interpreting."[10] The burden is on humans to make decisions without a guaranteed ethical guide. Cone appeals to Paul Tillich's view of Scripture, which orients the role and function of theological reflection about God. Since God cannot be described directly, symbols are used to point to dimensions of reality that cannot be spoken of literally. The Tillichian understanding of symbols does not only mean that blacks suffer as victims in a racist society but that "blackness" is an ontological symbol and a visible reality that most accurately represents what oppression means in America.

Since white Americans do not have the ability to recognize the humanity in persons of color, blacks need their own theology to affirm their identity in terms of a reality that is anti-black—blackness stands for all victims of white oppression. "White theology," when formed in isolation from the black experience, becomes a theology of white oppressors, serving as divine sanction for criminal acts committed against blacks. Cone argues that even those white theologians who try to connect theology to black suffering rarely utter a word that is relevant to the black experience in America. White theology is not Christian theology at all.[11] There is but one guiding principle of black theology: an unqualified commitment to

---

[9]Ibid., 3.
[10]Ibid., 7.
[11]Ibid., 9.

the black community as that community seeks to define its existence in light of God's liberating work in the world.

As such, black theology is a survival theology because it helps blacks navigate white-dominated American culture. In Cone's view, whites consider blacks animals, outside of the realm of humanity, and have attempted to destroy black identity through racial assimilation and integration programs, as if blacks have no legitimate existence apart from whiteness. Black theology is the theological expression of a people deprived of social and political power. In the victimologist vision, black liberation theology affirms being black in ways that white theology is simply incapable of affirming. Experience, in the end, is the ultimate guide because there is no such thing as objective truth. God is not the God of white religion but the God of black existence. In Cone's understanding, truth is not objective but subjective—a personal experience of the Ultimate in the midst of degradation.

THE ROLE OF THE BLACK EXPERIENCE

For Cone, the central reason for God's activity in the lives of human beings is to free them from political and economic oppression. If human relationships were not socially or politically oppressed, however, one might conjecture that according to black theology, Jesus' work would not be necessary. Black theology, then, is limited to "language about God's liberating activity in the world on behalf of the freedom of the oppressed."[12] Sociopolitical oppression is the core problem with the human community and is the central interpretive theme for all of black theology. The whole of the biblical story is, in fact, focused on God's "liberation of slaves from sociopolitical bondage."[13] This is the message of both the Old and New Testaments.

In the victimologist black identity, the evil intentions of others cause the vulnerable to live in poverty and oppression, requiring

---

[12]James H. Cone, *Speaking the Truth: Ecumenism, Liberation, and Black Theology* (Grand Rapids, MI: Eerdmans, 1986), 4.
[13]Ibid., 5.

action through the work and person of Christ. Poverty is viewed primarily as a direct result of oppression. Black liberation theologians are clear on this point: "People are poor because they are victims of others."[14] The social pathologies found in many black communities are viewed by black theologians as a result of past forms of oppression. Consistent with the victimologist vision, black theologians seek immediate solutions and remedies using language and themes related to social structural justice.

For blacks, as victims of oppression, even the worship experience in the church is uniquely tied to redefining their sense of being human within a context of marginalization. Cone notes, "Black people who have been humiliated and oppressed by the structures of white society six days of the week gather together each Sunday morning in order to experience another definition of their humanity."[15]

Both racism and socioeconomic oppression continue to augment the fragmentation between whites and blacks.[16] Historically speaking, it makes sense that black theologians would struggle with conceptualizing social justice and the problem of evil as it relates to the history of colonialism and slavery in the Americas.[17] The victimologist approach of black theology looks to explain and remedy a history of injustice by focusing on three components of autonomous black consciousness: slavery, racism, and structural change. The following sections will explore black liberation theology's perspective on these three issues before we identify any challenges to the black liberation motif.

SLAVERY

Slavery continues to be a historical starting point for reflecting on the role, function, and nature of black theology in America.

[14]Dwight N. Hopkins, *Heart and Head: Black Theology—Past, Present, and Future* (New York: Palgrave, 2002), 56.
[15]Cone, *Speaking the Truth*, 19.
[16]Dale P. Andrews, *Practical Theology for Black Churches: Bridging Black Theology and African American Folk Religion* (Louisville: Westminster John Knox Press, 2002), 93.
[17]William R. Jones, *Is God a White Racist? A Preamble to Black Theology* (Garden City, NY: Anchor Press, 1973).

Additionally, slavery remains one of the key factors in the plight of black America, significantly influencing how Christianity is practiced by blacks today. The focus on the issue of slavery by black liberation theologians makes sense, given the fact that Christianity was introduced to blacks in the Americas in the context of slave trading and slaveholding. Albert J. Raboteau contends, "From the very beginning of the Atlantic slave trade, conversion of the slaves to Christianity was viewed by the emerging nations of Western Christendom as a justification for enslavement of Africans."[18] Cone introduces the background of black religious thought by noting:

> Black religious thought has been primarily Christian, but strongly influenced by its African background and the struggle of black people to liberate themselves from slavery and second-class citizenship in North America. Because it has been developed in response to the involuntary servitude of Africans and subsequent black struggle for equality in the United States, it has never been exclusively Christian or primarily concerned with the explication of creeds and doctrines as found in the dominant theologies of Europe and America.[19]

In black religious thought, the theme of slavery is required for understanding the justice of God. In Cone's words, black Christians must deal with the existential agony of the question, "Why did God permit millions of blacks to be stolen from Africa and enslaved in a strange land?"[20]

Black Christianity received its distinctive "identity within the context of European enslavement of black people."[21] In 1693 Cotton Mather developed the Society of Negroes to give religious instruction to slaves, and a few years later, in 1702, efforts began in the South to Christianize slaves.[22] Because of their African roots, blacks first practiced a syncretistic Christianity, mixing traditional

---

[18]Albert J. Raboteau, *Slave Religion: The "Invisible Institution" in the Antebellum South* (Oxford: Oxford University Press, 2004), 96–288. See also Albert J. Raboteau, *Canaan Land: A Religious History of African Americans* (Oxford: Oxford University Press, 2001), 3–20.
[19]Cone, *Speaking the Truth*, 83.
[20]Ibid., 85.
[21]Ibid.
[22]Anne H. Pinn and Anthony B. Pinn, *Fortress Introduction to Black Church History* (Minneapolis: Fortress Press, 2002), 3–6.

African religions with Christianity.[23] This intermixing had a strong influence on worship forms.[24] Over time, however, the African religious elements were minimized, and Christianity was used as an opiate to suppress African elements in slave life.[25] As a result, black religious thought is "neither exclusively Christian" nor "primarily African."[26] Instead, it is "reinterpreted for and adapted to the life-situation of black people's struggle for justice in a nation whose social, political, and economic structures are dominated by a white racist ideology."[27]

Slavery, then, renders black religious thought unique and inaccessible to some, according to many black liberation theologians. Cone believes that "if religion is inseparably connected with life, then one must assume that slaves' and slaveholders' religious experiences did not have the same meaning because they did not share the same life. . . . [T]heir social and political realities were radically different."[28] Slavery, with its legacy of racism, is one of the reasons for the formation and continuation of black liberation theology.

RACISM

From the beginning, black theologians have struggled to comprehend the race question as it relates to white theologians. One of the central public roles of the black church has been to condemn all injustice, especially racism.[29] From slavery to reconstruction to the Jim Crow era and beyond, blacks in the United States have experienced a particular kind of racism. There has been some debate among scholars as to whether the African slave trade was motivated exclusively by race or if other motives were involved. Clarifying this could either indict or exonerate some Christians from the charge

---

[23]Hans Baer, *The Black Spiritual Movement: A Religious Response to Racism* (Knoxville, TN: University of Tennessee Press, 1984), 110–159.
[24]Edward D. Smith, *Climbing Jacob's Ladder: The Rise of Black Churches in Eastern Cities, 1740–1877* (Washington, D.C.: Smithsonian Institution Press, 1988), 24–25.
[25]Cone, *Speaking the Truth*, 86.
[26]Ibid.
[27]Ibid.
[28]Ibid., 87.
[29]Peter J. Paris, "The Public Role of the Black Churches," in *The Church's Public Role: Retrospect and Prospect*, ed. Deiter T. Hessel (Grand Rapids, MI: Eerdmans, 1993), 49.

of complicit participation in the slave trade. For example, Lakey argues that black slavery in the Americas was different from all other forms of slavery in world history because it was based on skin color alone and not on war captives, debts, punishment for crime, class, religion, culture, and so on.[30] For some, if race alone was the motivation for the slave trade, that exposes a deep-seated racism in the West that may still need to be addressed. Whatever the situation, the legacy of slavery seems to be the key factor in the pervasiveness of racism in America.

During slavery, white supremacy and slave ownership were mainstays of Calvinist and Puritan religious communities; even religious leaders such as Jonathan Edwards owned slaves.[31] However, during the Reconstruction era, some white Christians made efforts toward racial reconciliation. Primarily, though, the tendency among whites was toward racial segregation.[32] Riggins R. Earl Jr. highlights a critical distinction in the Christian identity of some racists by noting that white deists tended toward racism, while white theists tended to fight against discrimination.[33]

It was the racial strife of the nineteenth and twentieth centuries that led Cone and others to be suspicious of white Christians and whites in general. For example, in cities such as Birmingham, "Whites assumed blacks were irresponsible and unreliable and prone to commit crimes, especially crimes of passion."[34] Whites also resented the competition from blacks in the low-skilled labor market, resulting in many racist policies and race-based protests against blacks.[35] In early twentieth-century Philadelphia, black pastors organized the

---

[30]Othal Hawthorn Lakey, *The History of the CME Church* (Memphis: CME Publishing, 1985), 58.
[31]See Joseph R. Washington Jr., *Anti-Blackness in English Religion 1500–1800* (New York: Edwin Mellon Press, 1984), 309–311 and Joseph R. Washington Jr., *Puritan Race Virtue, Vice and Values 1620–1820: Original Calvinist True Believers' Enduring Faith and Ethics Race Claims (in Emerging Congregationalist, Presbyterian and Baptist Power Denominations* (New York: Peter Lang, 1987).
[32]Janet Duitsman Cornelius, *Slave Missions and the Black Church in the Antebellum South* (Columbia, SC: University of South Carolina Press, 1999), 205.
[33]Riggins R. Earl Jr., "Race, Suffering, Slavery, and Divine Providence: Some Black and White Nineteenth-Century Deists' and Theists' Voices," in *Christian Faith Seeking Historical Understanding,* ed. James O. Duke and Anthony L. Dunnavant (Macon, GA: Mercer University Press, 1997), 113–133.
[34]Wilson Fallin, *The African American Church in Birmingham, Alabama, 1815–1963: A Shelter in the Storm* (New York: Garland Publishing, 1997), 23–24.
[35]Ibid., 24.

Colored Protective Society to help combat the race riots that had been launched in protest of an increasing number of blacks moving to the city.[36] During the civil rights era and beyond, black Christians formed many parachurch groups, such as the Southern Christian Leadership Conference (SCLC), People United to Save Humanity (PUSH), and the Opportunities Industrialization Center (OIC), specifically to combat white racism and structural sins.[37]

Historically, white discrimination and racism among Christians have played important roles in the formation of separate black churches.[38] For example, the African Methodist Episcopal Church was started in Philadelphia in response to the racist actions of white Methodists. In one incident, Richard Allen and other black worshippers were pulled from their knees at St. George's Methodist Episcopal Church in Philadelphia because they were praying in a section that they did not know was closed to black Christians.[39] Generally speaking, Cone and others see very little progress with respect to race relations in the church:

> What deepens my anger today is the appalling silence of white theologians on racism in the United States and the modern world. Whereas this silence has been partly broken in secular disciplines, theology remains virtually mute. From Jonathan Edwards to Walter Rauschenbusch and Reinhold Niebuhr to the present, progressive white theologians, with few exceptions, write and teach as if they do not need to address the radical contradiction that racism creates for Christian theology. . . . White supremacy is so widespread that it becomes a "natural" way of viewing the world. We must ask therefore: Is racism so deeply embedded in Euro-American history and culture that it is impossible to do theology without being anti-black?[40]

---

[36]Robert Gregg, *Sparks from the Anvil of Oppression: Philadelphia's African Methodists and Southern Migrants* (Philadelphia: Temple University Press, 1993), 63.

[37]Emmanuel McCall, "The Black Church and Social Justice," in *Issues in Christian Ethics*, ed. Paul D. Simmons (Nashville: Broadman Press, 1980), 197–212.

[38]Eddie S. Glaude, *Religion, Race, and Nation in Early Nineteenth-Century Black America* (Chicago: University of Chicago Press, 2000), 24.

[39]C. Eric Lincoln and Lawrence H. Mamiya, *The Black Church in the African American Experience* (Durham, NC: Duke University Press, 1990), 50–51. Additionally, "Whites Only" sections were quite common in white churches.

[40]James H. Cone, *Risks of Faith: The Emergence of Black Theology of Liberation, 1968–1998* (Boston: Beacon Press, 1999), 130–131.

Cone believed that white supremacy and an orientation to all things "white have stretched the globe," with no people of color able to escape its cultural, political, and economic domination.[41] As Cone saw it, seminary and divinity school professors have contributed to America's white nationalist perspective by openly advocating the superiority of the white race over all others.[42] Although Cone believed that modern white theologians do not make their racist perspectives obvious in print, "their racism is concealed or unconscious. As long as religion scholars do not engage racism in their intellectual work, we can be sure that they are as racist as their grandparents, whether they know it or not."[43] Racism is so deeply intertwined in the fabric of American history and culture that "we cannot simply get rid of this cancer by ignoring it."[44] For Cone, to remain silent about America's racist past is implicit affirmation of racism as good and reveals a certain blindsidedness that leaves open the question of whether or not the church is equipped to address this issue.

However, the blame for the persistence of white racist theology partly falls to blacks. Cone believes that white theology's "amnesia about racism is due partly to the failure of black theologians to mount a persistently radical race critique of Christian theology—one so incisive and enduring that no one could do theology without engaging white supremacy in the modern world."[45] Even when black theologians were admitted to the faculties of predominantly white seminaries, churches, and other social institutions as tokens, "the radical edge of our race critique was quickly dropped as we enjoyed our newfound privileges."[46] According to Cone, white supremacy still exists in the academy and in our churches, and the remaining challenge for black theologians in the twenty-first century is "to develop an enduring race critique that is so comprehensively woven into Christian understanding that no one will be able to forget the

---

[41]Ibid.
[42]Ibid.
[43]Ibid., 132.
[44]Ibid.
[45]Ibid., 133–134.
[46]Ibid.

horrible crimes of white supremacy in the modern world."[47] One of the enduring qualities of the black church in the United States has been its role in helping blacks to cope with "demonic racism destroying black America."[48] Even in a postmodern context, white supremacy lingers, though it has been obscured by political correctness and multiculturalism.[49]

Bruce Fields, an evangelical black scholar, believes that black theology has a role in continuing to teach evangelicals about the ongoing presence of racism. Because racism is a consequence of total depravity, it should be expected, to a degree. Fields believes that "what many of us are ignorant of—through self-deception at best, or in rebellion at worst—is the possibility of racist attitudes and actions." Fields contends that it is difficult to move beyond the practice of avoiding members of particular racial or ethnic groups in the name of preference to an analysis of the nature of the preference for one group over another. In predominantly white churches, we may find that we are truly "like our fathers," though we may not do the exact same things.[50] Fields reminds his "white brothers and sisters" that it is possible for them to be racist, even though they may not have enslaved anyone, lynched anyone, or personally said anything degrading to or about an African-American.[51] According to Fields, racism still exists in the evangelical church because people can give or deny what is needed by other people on the basis of the other's race.[52] In the absence of deep personal relationships between members of different races, those not of one's own race are often relegated to the status of objects. As a result, the depersonalized "never become persons who are allowed to identify blind spots, insensitivities, and inconsistencies in the subjectors."[53] In other words, outside of a truly integrated community of whites together with blacks, blacks become objects and are not granted the

---

[47]Ibid., 137.
[48]Pinn and Pinn, *Fortress Introduction to Black Church History*, 138.
[49]Hopkins, *Heart and Head*, 55.
[50]Bruce Fields, *Introducing Black Theology: Three Crucial Questions for the Evangelical Church* (Grand Rapids, MI: Baker Academic, 2001), 57.
[51]Ibid., 64.
[52]Ibid., 65.
[53]Ibid., 65–66.

credibility to speak to white inconsistencies, hindering the desired movement toward racial reconciliation.

James H. Evans finds that the question of the humanity of black people and others is still shrouded by racist associations. "Spanish-speaking people are characterized as lazy, Asians as untrustworthy, and black people as criminals," writes Evans.[54] Wiley believes the persistence of white racism requires the presence of black theology to help blacks see themselves as "primarily responsible for overcoming [their] oppression."[55] However, black theologian Peter Paris warns against the narrowness of looking to racism to explain all of the deficiencies of the black community, noting that some non-race-related issues may also contribute to current conditions.[56]

SOCIAL STRUCTURES

Consistent with the victimologist vision, Cone and others focus much attention on the racism inherent in social structures, including those in the church. Cone maintains that if white churches expect to be taken seriously with their claim to be of God, then they must begin to act against the social order and against the ecclesiastical structures that do not affirm the humanity of people of color.[57] If white churches claim to be Christian institutions, and "if Jesus Christ is the Lord of the church and the world as white confessions claim, then church institutions that claim the Christian identity must reflect their commitment to him in the congregational life of the church as well as in its political and social involvement in society."[58]

---

[54]Evans, *We Have Been Believers: An African-American Systematic Theology*, 100. Wilmore noted further that white racism against blacks has introduced extra challenges in black pastoral ministry because of the instances of mental illness "directly traceable to internalized frustration and rage induced by the effects of racism and oppression in the environment." See Gayraud S. Wilmore, "Pastoral Ministry in Black Theology," in *Black Theology: A Documentary History, Volume II: 1980–1992*, ed. James H. Cone and Gayraud S. Wilmore (Maryknoll, NY: Orbis Books, 1993), 121.
[55]Dennis W. Wiley, "The African-American Community," in *Black Theology: A Documentary History, Volume II*, 128.
[56]Paris, *The Social Teachings of the Black Churches*, 102.
[57]Cone, *Speaking the Truth*, 120.
[58]Ibid., 121.

Ideally, social involvement by Christians will have an impact on social structures in the church and the culture at large. George Yancey highlights the fact that structural sin operates freely in our society and affects the life of every minority.[59] Structural sins are born out of historical injustices where a society has built-in discrimination, regardless of whether individual members are racist.[60] For blacks, these structural forms of racism are found in residential segregation and in educational institutions of white preference.[61] Bruce Fields embraces black theology on this point, noting that "as a movement, [black theology] reminds the church of the pervasiveness of sin in systems, structures, and socio-political institutions."[62] Systemic and structural sins result in the perpetuation of "injustice to, and dehumanization of, select groups in socio-cultural constructs."[63]

Institutional racism continued after the civil rights movement as the next great evil to be tackled. Structural and institutional racism permits whites to maintain control over blacks; therefore, this type of racism must be eliminated in order to achieve true racial harmony in all sectors of society.[64] Fields, however, believes that evangelicals are suspicious of addressing structural issues for three reasons: (1) sociopolitical involvement may undermine orthodox doctrine; (2) some eschatological positions cause Christians to withdraw from culture and to incorporate a pessimistic attitude toward human culture and social involvement; and (3) our individualistic tendencies draw us away from a community consciousness that would aid us in identifying systemic and structural sin "because it gets our eyes off of ourselves."[65]

Cornel West maintains that black theology has not gone far enough in addressing structural sin. Early conceptions of black

---

[59]George A. Yancey, *Beyond Black and White: Reflections on Racial Reconciliation* (Grand Rapids, MI: Baker Books, 1996), 43.
[60]Ibid.
[61]Ibid., 43–47.
[62]Fields, *Introducing Black Theology*, 67.
[63]Ibid., 68.
[64]Mid-Peninsula Christian Ministry, "Institutional Racism in American Society," in *Moral Issues and Christian Response*, ed. Paul T. Jersild and Dale A. Johnson (New York: Holt, Rinehart, and Winston, 1971), 254–268.
[65]Fields, *Introducing Black Theology*, 69.

theology, according to West, had severe limitations in this area. West understands that the early limitations of black theology when addressing structural issues are to be found in

> [its] absence of a systematic social analysis, which has prevented black theologians from coming to terms with the relationships between racism, sexism, class exploitation and imperialist oppression . . . [and] its [black theology's] tendency to downplay existential issues such as death, disease, dread, despair and disappointment which are related to yet not identical with suffering caused by oppressive social structures.[66]

American society continues to be a place rife with racist structures.[67] Blacks continue to be victims of such structures in the areas of banking, mortgage appropriations, disability benefits, small business loans, education, and so on.[68]

Some black intellectuals, however, are moving toward a more honest look at the supposed oppression of blacks in an economic environment dominated by whites. In fact, black theologians such as William Jones note that blacks, as consumers, have an enormous amount of economic power. In a capitalist system, consumption is ultimately more determinative than production; therefore, black consumption power has more control over market processes than many people realize.[69] That is, blacks have more power and identity as a spending class in control of their own destiny than as a racial group alone.

In black theology, racism is seen primarily as a structural problem. As a result, Cone and others make indictments against the white church and white theologians because they represent not just individuals but the structural manifestation of what is wrong in black communities and in the black church.

---

[66]Cornel West, "Black Theology of Liberation as Critique of Capitalist Civilization," in *Black Theology: A Documentary History, Volume II*, 416.
[67]Sharon D. Welch, *Reconstructing Christian Theology* (Minneapolis: Fortress Press, 1994), 173–174.
[68]Ibid.
[69]William A. Jones, "Confronting the System," in *African American Religious Thought: An Interdisciplinary Anthology*, ed. Gayraud S. Wilmore (Durham, NC: Duke University Press, 1989), 441.

THE SOURCES AND NORMS OF BLACK THEOLOGY

Depending heavily on Karl Barth and Paul Tillich, Cone outlines the sources and the norms for black theology, the presuppositions that determine the questions that are to be asked as well as the answers that are to be given.[70] The sources and norms of black theology come out of the perspective of the black person as victim and, in Cone's view, must be independent from any corruptive influence of white thought. The sources are as follows:

(1) *The black experience:* Black theology derives and shapes its theology from the black experience in America, which is a life of humiliation and suffering. The black experience forces the black community to ask questions such as, "What does revelation mean when one's being is engulfed in a system of white racism cloaking itself in pious moralities? What does God mean when a police officer whacks you over the head because you are black? What does the church mean when white churchmen say they need more time to end racism?"[71]

(2) *Black history:* Black history refers to the way blacks were brought to this continent and the way they have been treated since. Cone specifically addresses the need to remember that blacks were considered nonpersons for most of their history in North America.

(3) *Black culture:* Black culture consists of the creative forms of expression as one reflects on history, endures pain, and experiences joy within the context of being an oppressed victim. God's revelation comes through the cultural situation of the oppressed.

(4) *Revelation:* Revelation is an event, a happening in human history. It is God's self-revelation to the human race through the historical act of human liberation. Jesus is the plenary revelation of God and comes to the black experience in the struggle for liberation.

(5) *Scripture:* Black theology is biblical theology. Since the Bible is not the revelation of God (only Jesus is), the Bible serves as a guide for checking the interpretation of God's revelation in light of a God

---

[70]Cone, *A Black Theology of Liberation*, 22.
[71]Ibid., 24.

who is a God of liberation, who speaks to the oppressed and abused and assures them that divine righteousness will vindicate their suffering. The Bible is not an infallible witness. God is not the author of the Bible, and any effort to prove verbal inspiration detracts from the real meaning of the biblical message: human liberation. The meaning of Scripture is not to be found in the words of the Scripture as such but only in its power to point beyond itself to the reality of God's revelation directed at black liberation.

(6) *Tradition:* Black theology focuses primarily on the history of the black church in America and secondarily on white western Christianity. It believes that the authentic Christian gospel, as expressed in the New Testament, is found more dominantly in the pre-Civil War black church than in its white counterpart. Concomitant with this tradition is the inherent theological understanding that the interpretation of the gospel directs theology in political, economic, and social liberation.[72]

The norm of black theology is the hermeneutical principle that is decisive in specifying how sources are used by rating their importance and by distinguishing relevant data from irrelevant, as Cone defines the terms. As such, the norm of black theology is the manifestation of Jesus as the black Christ who provides the necessary soul for black liberation. Jesus Christ is the one presently breaking the power of white racism, and Cone believes that this alone is the norm for black talk about God.

CONCLUSION

Much of Cone's rhetoric may sound overly harsh, but the context does provide helpful insight into the anger and frustration felt by Cone and other black church leaders at the end of the civil rights movement. Sadly, the pain and frustration of the injustices around theologians like Cone became an overcontrolling theme in their theological development. While the experience of oppression was a reality for many blacks during Cone's early years, reducing all

---

[72]Ibid., 23–35.

of theology to addressing issues like slavery and racism, structural oppression redirected the holistic imperative of the redemptive character of the gospel to all of life, not simply political and social life. With neoorthodoxy as a starting point, Cone and others, as shown in the chapters to follow, attempted to steer the black church in a direction intended to help but in the end created other significant problems.

3

Cone's Theological Scaffolding

In biblical history, there's not one word written in the Bible between Genesis and Revelations that was not written under one of six different kinds of oppression, Egyptian oppression, Assyrian oppression, Persian oppression, Greek oppression, Roman oppression, Babylonian oppression.

The Roman oppression is the period in which Jesus is born. And comparing imperialism that was going on in Luke, imperialism was going on when Caesar Augustus sent out a decree that the whole world should be taxed. They weren't in charge of the world. It sounds like some other governments I know.[1]

JEREMIAH WRIGHT

✝

The words of Jeremiah Wright were such a shock to many Christians that many Americans were wondering if black liberation theology was a stand-alone tradition or part of a theological system. To the surprise of many, black theologians over the years have tried to construct a cogent systematic theology around the idea of God liberating people from social oppression as a primary motif. Whether the attempt was successful or not is the subject of this chapter. The doctrines discussed in this chapter are described in contradistinction to the summary of historic positions of orthodoxy described in the first chapter. For many evangelicals, Cone's doctrinal formulations will seem foreign, but they provide the overall scaffolding not only

---

[1]"Reverend Wright at the National Press Club," *New York Times* (April 28, 2008); http://www.nytimes.com/2008/04/28/us/politics/28text-wright.html?_r=2&pagewanted=8.

for Cone's theology but for the next generation of black theologians to follow him.

CONE'S DOCTRINE OF GOD: GOD OF THE OPPRESSED

In 1970, Cone set the course for developing a doctrine of God in his book *A Black Theology of Liberation* and then later, in 1975, developed it more fully in the book *God of the Oppressed*.[2] Initially Cone described the hermeneutical principles that would be used to organize the formation of the doctrine for black theology. The first principle is that the Christian understanding of God arises from the biblical view of revelation, a revelation of God that takes place in the liberation of oppressed Israel and is completed in the incarnation of Christ. Second, the doctrine of God in black theology must describe a God who is participating in the liberation of the oppressed as decisively revealed in the Oppressed One, Jesus Christ. God became the Oppressed One so that he could liberate those who are victims of oppression. God is, in fact, black because God has made the oppressed condition his own condition.

Cone explains the doctrine of the Trinity in terms of God's essential blackness and identification with victims. In the Trinitarian view of the Godhead, black theology says that as Creator, God identified with oppressed Israel and participated in the forming of that people; as Redeemer, God became the Oppressed One so that all may be free from oppression; as Holy Spirit, God continues the work of liberation. The Holy Spirit is the Spirit of the Creator and Redeemer currently at work in society in the forces of human liberation. In America, the Holy Spirit aids blacks in making decisions about their togetherness, which means making preparation for an encounter with whites.

Again, God is the God of the oppressed in the Conian victimologist vision. Cone lays out his doctrine of God by orienting his view about the nature of God in view of God's self-disclosure in biblical

---

[2]James H. Cone, *A Black Theology of Liberation* (original edition: New York: Lippincott, 1970) and *God of the Oppressed* (San Francisco: Harper Collins, 1975).

history, as well as in the oppressed condition of black Americans.[3] The poor, whom Jesus came to liberate, "were not those spiritually poor, as suggested in Matthew 5:3," but rather those who were materially poor and persecuted.[4] In Cone's view, the poor are the oppressed victims—those who cannot defend themselves against the powerful and who are in need of an advocate, liberator, and protector.[5] The poor are

> the least and the last, the hungry and thirsty, the unclothed and the strangers, the sick and captives. It is for these little ones that the gospel is preached and for whom liberation has come in the words and deeds of Jesus . . . it is important to point out that Jesus does not promise to include the poor in the Kingdom *along with* others who may be rich and learned. His promise is that the Kingdom belongs to the poor *alone*.[6]

The gospel excludes those who stand outside of the reality of poverty and oppression.[7] Christ becomes poor for the poor; he becomes oppressed for the oppressed. He becomes the victim and transforms the condition of slavery into the platform for the struggle for freedom.[8] The resurrection frees oppressed victims and empowers them to pursue their humanity. Therefore, to understand the historical Jesus outside of his identification with the poor is to distort his person and work.[9] Jesus was born into an oppressed community and baptized into a poor community. He ministered to and identified with the poor. Jesus was a victim of social and structural oppression by cultural elites. He died and was resurrected into complete freedom as "the Oppressed One" who reveals that God is present in all dimensions of human liberation.[10]

---

[3] Cone, *A Black Theology of Liberation* (Maryknoll, NY: Orbis Books, 1990), 55.
[4] Ibid., 79.
[5] Ibid.
[6] Ibid.
[7] Ibid.
[8] Ibid., 81.
[9] Ibid., 113.
[10] Ibid., 114–119. Dwight N. Hopkins, *Heart and Head: Black Theology—Past, Present, and Future* (New York: Palgrave, 2002), 54–57 admits that postmodernity has diluted the focus on God's preferential option for the poor. Postmodernity, notes Hopkins, "emphasizes the lack of foundations in life, the lack of absolute justice, and the lack of clarity on right and wrong." This lack of conviction has led ethicists away from focusing on absolute justice. Hopkins reinforces

In America, Jesus Christ should be referred to as the "Black Christ" by all Christians because of his mission to save oppressed victims who are black.[11] In black theology, it is the oppressed community that determines the meaning and scope of Jesus' message.[12] The call of Moses and the missiological declaration of Christ reveal God's liberating intentions in the context of a people who suffer under the yoke of oppression.[13] "The black community," says Cone, "is an oppressed community primarily because of its blackness; hence, the christological importance of Jesus must be found in his blackness. If he is not black as we are, then the resurrection has little significance for our times."[14] It is Christ's shared victimology that uniquely binds him to blacks who have suffered under centuries of oppression by whites.

Black Christian identity is dependent on Christ's being present in the oppressed black condition, revealing to blacks what is necessary for liberation.[15] In Christ, God becomes oppressed humanity—a humanity, in America, that is black. Calling Christ black "means that black people are God's poor people whom Christ had come to liberate."[16] Christ is black not because of cultural preferences but because of the fact that he literally entered into the world "where the poor, the despised, and the black are, disclosing that he is with them, enduring their humiliation and pain and transforming oppressed slaves into liberated servants."[17] The black Christ leads "the warfare against the white assault on blackness by striking white values and white religion."[18] The black Christ challenges

---

the idea that God prefers the poor because God opposes all forms of injustice that block the full humanity of the most vulnerable in society. Hopkins seeks to continue the emphasis on God's activity with the poor because Scripture teaches that "people are poor because they are victims of others." Additionally, the Bible calls the human family to oppose poverty because God specifically moves to hear the "cries of slaves, the poor, and working people." God works on their behalf to liberate them from oppression and place them in a context of realized humanity. The social locations of the poor matter to God.

[11] Kelly Brown Douglas, *The Black Christ* (Maryknoll, NY: Orbis Books, 1994).

[12] Cone, *Black Theology of Liberation*, 119. The implication here is that he does not identify with whites who have had a historical relationship on the side of oppressors.

[13] James H. Evans Jr., *We Have Been Believers: An African-American Systematic Theology* (Minneapolis: Fortress Press, 1992), 11.

[14] Cone, *A Black Theology of Liberation*, 120.

[15] Ibid.

[16] Ibid., 136.

[17] Cone, *God of the Oppressed*, 136.

[18] Ibid., 121.

the structures of evil as seen in white society, rebelling against it and demonstrating what black Christians must become.[19] "The passive Christ of white Christianity when combined with African culture became the Liberator of oppressed victims from socio-political oppression," writes Cone.[20]

Following a black Christ means that blacks must refuse to let whites define what is appropriate for the black community.[21] Moreover, the resurrection of Christ is understood by black theologians as a political event. The resurrection grants freedom to the poor—to those who, through Christ, discover that their poverty is traceable to the rich and powerful in this world.[22] The resurrection requires that the poor practice political activity against the social and economic structures that make them poor; to do otherwise is to deny the freedom of the resurrection.[23]

THE HERMENEUTICS OF OPPRESSION

The implications for hermeneutics in black theology require that all exegesis be grounded in the presupposition of God in Christ as the liberator of oppressed victims. A theology developed in light of Christ's liberating activity must be based on the following four guidelines: (1) There can be no Christian theology that is not social and political; (2) theology cannot simply repeat what the Bible says or what is found in a particular theological tradition; (3) theology cannot ignore cultural tradition; and (4) theology is always about the liberation of oppressed victims.[24] It is important to remember that for Cone, only two populations exist in the world—namely, the oppressed and the oppressors. By extension, then, the social determination necessary for faith in God's work of liberation is present in the social condition of the poor in a way that it is not present in the rich.[25] Here Cone is content with the charge that social ideol-

---

[19]Ibid.
[20]Ibid., 114.
[21]Ibid., 122.
[22]Ibid., 125.
[23]Ibid.
[24]Ibid., 82–83.
[25]Ibid., 95.

ogy influences theological understanding, but his main concern is *whose* theological understanding—i.e., the oppressors in their social context or the oppressed victims who are longing for freedom from victimization. Again, grounded in victim-oriented black consciousness, one's method of biblical interpretation will begin and end with a particular interpretation of the black experience.

Cone rejects the charge that black theology can be reduced simply to black politics, but he affirms that Christian theology begins and ends with revelation. However, this revelation is the story of God as he liberates his people from oppression. White theology, therefore, is an ideological distortion of the gospel because it is not grounded in the liberating activity of oppression.[26] To Cone, "white theologians" come not from a history of oppression but rather from a tradition of oppressors. Moreover, because the values of white culture are antithetical to biblical revelation, "it is impossible to be white (culturally speaking) and also think biblically. . . . [B]iblical thinking is *liberated* thought." In other words, biblical thinking is not constrained to the worldview of the dominant culture.[27] To think biblically is to think in light of liberating oppressed victims. The overall task of theology is "to show the significance of the struggle of the oppressed against inhuman powers, relating to people's struggle with God's intention to set them free."[28]

Cone believes that it is impossible to be truthful about theology if it is disconnected from our life experience. "As long as we live and have our being in time and space," he writes, "absolute truth is impossible."[29] What transcends all, in Cone's view, is the use of story. "Story" is the history of "individuals coming together in the struggle to shape life according to commonly held values."[30] The white American story is one of European settlements "struggling against dark forces and savage people" to establish a new nation.

---

[26]Ibid., 97.
[27]Ibid., italics his.
[28]Ibid., 99.
[29]Ibid., 102.
[30]Ibid.

The black American story is "recorded in the songs, tales, and narratives of African slaves and their descendants, as they attempted to survive with dignity."[31]

Since truth is inseparable from story, any objectivity in thought is achieved only through subjectivity. Truth is an event that happens "to" us, often "against" our will.[32] In black religion, story produces two forms of truth: (1) There is the story of black people as a whole—a story that dates back to the transatlantic slave trade, through slavery, reconstruction, and the Jim Crow era; and (2) there is another story that moves beyond the corporate—one's personal story. Personal stories are accounts of individual victories within the context of struggle.[33] To give validity to the authority of story, Cone grounds his position in "a story about a man called Jesus."[34] Grounding Christianity in the narrative of Christ's work establishes the authority of story.

CONE'S DOCTRINE OF SCRIPTURE

Cone remains critical of an orthodox evangelical theology that maintains the infallibility and inerrancy of the Scriptures and the Creator/creature distinction and holds the Scriptures as the final authority for all matters of faith, because those positions fail to uncover issues important to "the wretched of the earth."[35] In the Conian framework, if revelation is not related to black liberation, it has no value and is to be rejected.[36] There can simply be no genuine reflection of God and man outside of discussing the liberation of oppressed victims.[37] Scripture came out of a community of oppression and is directed at the human person as such. Scripture functions to serve the issues that are raised in the victimized experience that has formed black consciousness in America.

Cone believes there is no perfect guide for discerning God's

---

[31]Ibid.
[32]Ibid., 105.
[33]Ibid., 105–106.
[34]Ibid., 106.
[35]Ibid., 83.
[36]Ibid.
[37]Ibid.

movement in the world. In fact, he asserts that "contrary to what many conservatives would say, the Bible is not a blueprint on this matter. It is a valuable symbol for pointing to God's revelation in Jesus, but it is not self-interpreting. We are thus placed in an existential situation of freedom in which the burden is on us to make decisions without a guaranteed ethical guide."[38]

Extrabiblical sources, such as ideas found in the writings of Karl Marx and Ludwig Feuerbach, are believed to provide a more sufficient source for addressing the issues facing black Christians. Marxism is more sufficient than Scripture for interpreting, evaluating, and understanding reality in the Conian framework. For example, Cone explains that "the Christian faith does not possess in its nature the means for analyzing the structure of capitalism. Marxism as a tool of social analysis can disclose the gap between appearance and reality, and thereby help Christians to see how things really are."[39] Cone believes that Marx's chief contribution is "his disclosure of the ideological character of bourgeois thought, indicating the connections between the 'ruling *material* force of society' and the 'ruling *intellectual*' force.'"[40] In this framework, intellectual ideas emerge out of a definitive context—and a socially constructed point of view. Cone praises Marx for noting that truth is a question "not only of what is but of what ought to be."[41] The definition of reality is determined by the "existing societal relations of material production, with the ruling class controlling the means of production as well as the intellectual forces which justify the present political arrangements."[42] In Marxism, the "oughts" of human community are defined by what can be accomplished through the "revolutionary praxis of the proletarian class, overthrowing unjust societal conditions."[43] Marx's thought is useful and attractive to Cone because it allows black theologians to

---

[38]Cone, *A Black Theology of Liberation*, 7.
[39]James H. Cone, *For My People: Black Theology and the Black Church* (Maryknoll, NY: Orbis Books, 1984), 187.
[40]Cone, *God of the Oppressed*, 41, italics his.
[41]Ibid., 42.
[42]Ibid.
[43]Ibid.

critique racism in America on the basis of victimology, power, and revolution.[44]

Marxists believe that the promotion of religion by the ruling class reveals a conspiracy to sanction materialism and jade the proletariat, leaving it content with humiliation and suffering. With this in mind, Cone raises several important questions that theologians must ask in light of Marx's truth. For example, "What is the connection between dominant material relations and the ruling theological ideas in a given society?"[45] Taking Marx seriously, remarks Cone, will make theologians "confess their limitations, their inability to say anything about God which is not at the same time a statement about the social context of their own existence."[46] Using other sources must be the case because, according to Cone and others, there is no objectivity in theology. Although the revelation of God may be universal, Cone writes, "Theological talk about that revelation is filtered through human experience, which is limited by their social realities."[47] For Cone, integrating Marx into black theology helps theologians perceive just how social perceptions determine theological questions and conclusions. Moreover, these questions and answers are "largely a reflection of the material condition of a given society."[48] Theologians, in the end, must face the fact that their enterprise is merely a reflection of social conditioning. Because of this, neither white nor black theology can avoid the interplay between theology and society. Cone summarizes his reflections on Marx by noting that "what people think about God, Jesus Christ, and the Church cannot be separated from their own social and political status in a given society."[49]

Cone uses his gleanings from Marx (and other German Socialists) to launch a full-scale critique of what he calls "white American

---

[44]African liberation theologians also find Marxism to be a useful tool in evaluating the history of racism and colonialism. See Itumeleng J. Mosala and Buti Tlahagle, eds., *The Unquestionable Right to Be Free: Black Theology in South Africa* (Maryknoll, NY: Orbis Books, 1986), 29.

[45]Cone, *God of the Oppressed*, 42.

[46]Ibid., 43.

[47]Ibid.

[48]Ibid.

[49]Ibid., 45.

theology."[50] Cone's earliest assessments of "white" theologians revolve around his belief that "white socio-political interests" drive the theological exposition of Caucasian theologians. "White" Christian theology thus systematically excludes blacks because their social existence has never been of value to white theologians. Cone uses a Marxist class analysis to conclude that because most professional theologians are descendants of the advantaged class and thus often represent the consciousness of the class, "it is difficult not to conclude that their theologies are in fact a bourgeois exercise in intellectual masturbation."[51] In other words, mainstream theology is written by the advantaged class and is for the advantaged class only. For Cone, "American theology" only confirms Marx's contention that their ideas are simply by-products of a commitment to maintaining a bourgeois existence.

Employing a Marxist critical lens, Cone finds that Protestant historical theology from "Cotton Mather and Jonathan Edwards to Reinhold Niebuhr and Schubert Ogden, including radicals and conservatives, have interpreted the gospel according to the cultural and political interests of white people."[52] Because white American theologians are limited within white power structures, they are also limited in their depth of insight. As proof of his claim, Cone cites historical mainstream support for (or lack of comment on) American chattel slavery by many Presbyterians, Congregationalists, Baptists, Methodists, and others.[53] For example, Cone wonders how a theologian as great as Jonathan Edwards could preach great sermons but never mention issues related to slavery.[54] Further, how could Presbyterians, Methodists, and Baptists actually defend and support slavery?

Cone raises the issue of Christian orthodox support of slavery and social injustice only out of his concern "with the essence of Christian theology and the influences of culture on a theologian's

---

[50]Ibid., 39–45.
[51]Ibid., 47.
[52]Ibid.
[53]Ibid.
[54]Ibid. Even more puzzling for some is how Edwards could be a slave owner himself.

understanding of the theological task."[55] In the end, because white theologians do not live in a society that is racist against them, the oppression of blacks does not occupy an important place in their theology.[56] Because white theologians represent the interests of those who control the means of production, they are more concerned about issues in systematic theology than about issues of social ethics.

In fairness, Cone confesses that black theology also reflects a particular cultural context, but "unlike white theologians, who spoke to and for the culture of the ruling class, black people's religious ideas were shaped by the cultural and political existence of the victims of North America."[57] It is the victimology expressed in this form of black consciousness that drives the paradigm for black theology.

Cone suggests using different theological categories to understand the nature of God in an effort to throw off the distinctions that were not created from the black experience.[58] Cone, however, is careful to reject the atheism of Marxism by disagreeing with those blacks who have accepted a Marxist understanding of the role and function of religion "without probing deeper into the thought forms of black people."[59] For slaves who first heard the gospel on plantations that were owned and operated by white Christians, it was precisely the work and person of Christ presented in the preaching and teaching of the Scriptures that provided "a knowledge of themselves."[60] It follows, then, that Jesus is confirmed by God in his "blackness" to bring good news to liberate oppressed victims, in complete contradiction to Marx's observation regarding the oppressive dimensions of religion.[61]

Cone seeks to go beyond Marx, noting that while Marx is helpful, the problem of oppression is "much more complex" than

---

[55]Ibid., 51.
[56]Ibid., 52. Cone quotes Marx as saying, "It is not consciousness that determines life, but life that determines consciousness."
[57]Ibid., 53.
[58]Ibid., 124.
[59]Ibid., 130.
[60]Ibid.
[61]Ibid., 136.

he envisioned.[62] Cone firmly believes that an analysis that "fails to deal with racism, that demon embedded in white folks' being, is inadequate."[63] Black theology exists as a correction to *"theologians of the Christian church* [who] *have not interpreted Christian ethics as an act for the liberation of the oppressed because their views of divine revelation were defined by philosophy and other cultural values rather than by the biblical theme of God as liberator of the oppressed."*[64] American theologians would have written differently, Cone asserts, if Scripture had been interpreted through the eyes of oppressed victims rather than through the eyes of white privilege. Marxist thought in black theology will receive specific attention later in this book.

CONE'S ANTHROPOLOGY

Cone's anthropology begins and ends with the experience of the human person in relation to other persons, not as a creature created by a triune God. The entire corpus of James Cone's writing focuses on oppression and white racism. Therefore, his anthropological perspective deals primarily with reflection as related to social injustice, racism, and oppression.

Cone explains his anthropology in terms of redeeming persons who were once used by oppressors to dehumanize Africans and African-Americans in particular. In addition, other minorities, women, and practicing homosexuals were dehumanized by oppressors as well. While Cone does have a sense of the moral limitations of the human person, he tends to deal with those limitations systemically and structurally rather than focusing on them individually or personally. In terms of anthropology, Cone's perspective coheres nicely with the victimologist vision.

The normative oppression of blacks within the context of United States history, for both Cone and others, makes anthropological issues of paramount importance. Because of the devaluation

---

[62]Ibid., 156.
[63]Ibid.
[64]Ibid., 200, italics his.

of the humanity of non-Anglo races by whites, black liberation theologians have spent considerable energy applying the *imago Dei* to African-Americans. As Cone notes, "The extermination of Amerindians, the persecution of the Jews, the oppression of Mexican-Americans, and every other conceivable inhumanity done in the name of God and country . . . can be analyzed in terms of the white American inability to recognize humanity in people of color."[65] Affirming black identity, as well as the identities of all people of color, is the focus of black theology. What people of color need, in the end, is liberation from white dehumanization that is systemically and structurally executed.

Cone is plagued by seeking to reconcile Christian theology with the black consciousness designated as victim. For example, he asks, "What about depriving blacks of their humanity by suggesting that white humanity is humanity as God intended it to be? What about the liberal emphasis on human goodness at the same time whites were doing everything they could to destroy blacks?"[66] Black theology begins, then, with the black condition as the starting point for understanding human experience. Black theology will "illuminate the black condition so that blacks can see that their liberation is the manifestation of God's activity."[67] The very definition of the human person must be limited to "what it means to be liberated from human oppression."[68] In the end, in black theology the structural issues are the significant ones for evaluation, and this focus orients black theology into the American experience of blacks as victims.

If the starting point of the gospel and theology is human liberation, it becomes important, then, to describe exactly what people are being liberated from. For black theology, freedom is the hermeneutical hinge from which Christian anthropology swings. Freedom is essential to what it means to be human and is the first principle in knowing what it means to be a human person. Cone outlines five relationships of freedom from victimization in theology: (1) freedom

---

[65]Cone, *A Black Theology of Liberation*, 7.
[66]Ibid., 83.
[67]Ibid., 85.
[68]Ibid., 87.

as liberation from oppression; (2) freedom and the image of God; (3) freedom as identification with an oppressed community; (4) freedom and suffering; and (5) freedom and blackness.

First, in the Conian view, freedom is defined as liberation from oppression. Cone maintains, "The liberated, the free, are the ones who define the meaning of their being in terms of the oppressed of the land by participating in their liberation."[69] Freedom is seen as the opposite of oppression, and being truly human means to be "identified with those who are enslaved as they fight against human oppression."[70] The emphasis, again, is on the structural relationship between groups. Cone depends heavily on the work of Karl Marx to explain that liberating activity involves dealing with the social structures that led to the oppression of some and not others.[71]

Second, the *imago Dei* is not neglected in Cone's view of anthropology. While Cone appreciates some aspects of the traditional understanding of this concept, he argues that the traditional view is too limited. Although Cone acknowledges that freedom is central to comprehending what it means to be made in God's image, this understanding fails to "place due emphasis on the role of liberation in an oppressive society."[72] Instead, Cone maintains, "The biblical concept of image means that human beings are created in such a way that they cannot obey oppressive laws and still be human."[73] To be human is to be made in the image of God, "revolting against everything that is opposed to humanity."[74] As God is centrally interested in liberation, his image-bearers will bear the same burden as well. In Cone's view, the image of God implies that the human person will work against the oppression of others. Simply stated, in a world of oppression, "the image is human nature in rebellion against the structures of oppression."[75] The *imago Dei* is the image of the human person as victim.

---

[69]Ibid.
[70]Ibid., 87–88.
[71]Ibid., 89.
[72]Ibid., 93.
[73]Ibid.
[74]Ibid.
[75]Ibid., 94.

Third, Cone is quick to point out that freedom should not be understood in terms of "white middle-class individualism."[76] This type of freedom enables individuals to do whatever they wish without the coercion of others. Instead, Cone asserts, "persons are free when they belong to a free community seeking to emancipate itself from oppression."[77] Freedom is not libertinism; rather, it "always involves making decisions within the context of a community of persons who share similar goals and are seeking the same liberation. Freedom is taking sides . . . when a society is divided into oppressed and oppressors."[78] Freedom involves committing one's whole existence to the liberation of those who are under oppression. In order to be free, a person must be able to make decisions and choices that are not dependent on an oppressive system.[79] Whites, in the end, are not free to offer prescriptions about issues in the black community because they are not members of an oppressed community. Until whites have experienced oppression, they are not capable of commenting on the future of African-American progress.

Fourth, freedom is always associated with suffering. Cone writes, "To assert one's freedom always involves encountering the economic and social structures of oppression."[80] Living in America, in Cone's view, has been an absurd experience for blacks, one demanding a key decision that blacks "either accept their place or resolve to call down upon themselves white indignation by revolting against the world as it is."[81] Cone promotes the idea that blacks should do whatever is necessary to alleviate their corporate suffering and move toward freedom. Cone ultimately appeals to Scripture to ground the idea that freedom is bound up with suffering. Jesus chose a life of suffering to redeem those who suffer. Cone notes not only that Jesus limited the kingdom to poor and unwanted victims

---

[76]Ibid.
[77]Ibid.
[78]Ibid., 94–95.
[79]Ibid., 96.
[80]Ibid., 97.
[81]Ibid., 99.

but also that the kingdom is "for the poor because they represent the meaning of oppression and the certainty of liberation."[82]

Fifth, freedom affirms genuine blackness. Blackness is both "the symbol of oppression and of the certainty of liberation"; so "freedom means an affirmation of blackness. To be free is to be black—that is, identified with the victims of humiliation in human society and a participant in the liberation of oppressed humanity."[83] Freedom must affirm blackness because whiteness results in oppression and human affliction. Whiteness is the enemy to be slain. When black individuals value their blackness and view it as bound with suffering, they can move into fighting for liberation. When blacks affirm and glory in their freedom to be black and reject white dehumanization and oppression, they "not only liberate themselves from oppression, but they also liberate oppressors from enslavement to their illusions."[84]

CONE'S VIEWS ON SIN AND REDEMPTION

Cone defines sin as "separation from the source of being."[85] In this understanding, the source of being is God. This definition—and Cone's theology in general—echoes the twentieth-century liberal Protestant tradition. Cone believes that humans sin when instead of affirming their identity in the source of being, they reject their identity and attempt to be what they are not. Sin, in Cone's view, is defined as being in relation to nonbeing as a condition of estrangement from the source of meaning and purpose in the universe. Sin is a religious concept that defines the human condition as separated from the essence of the community. To be in sin, says Cone, has nothing to do with disobeying objective laws that are alien to the community's existence but is living according to selfish interests rather than according to what is best for the community.

Consistent with a victimologist vision of blacks, Cone initially develops a definition of sin in its corporate or structural form. First,

---

[82]Ibid., 101.
[83]Ibid.
[84]Ibid., 103.
[85]Cone, *God of the Oppressed*, 103.

he describes sin as a community concept. Sin, ultimately, has meaning only within the context of human relationships. For Cone, sin was introduced as meaningful only "within the context of the Israelite community."[86] To be considered living in sin, one must "deny the values that make the community what it is."[87] This concept of sin, Cone affirms, has federal implications in that this condition applies to all human beings. So the entire Israelite community found itself in sin because Israel failed to "recognize the liberating work of God" before Mount Sinai.[88] Sin involves believing that liberation is not God's primary task. Failing to recognize and participate in the liberating work of God as revealed in Christ is to live in sin.

Second, in terms of relationships between whites and blacks, sin cannot be understood properly in a white context because it "is a concept that is meaningful only for an oppressed community as it reflects upon liberation."[89] As whites are not members of an oppressed community, they cannot rightly understand the concept of sin. Moreover, knowledge of sinful humanity cannot even exist "except in the movement of an oppressed community claiming its freedom."[90] By implication, whites are incapable of understanding sin and should refrain from speaking about it within the black community. Cone calls for a "destruction of whiteness, which is the source of human misery in the world."[91] This view of sin, then, in Cone's victimologist vision, results in different definitions of sin for blacks and for whites. Cone laments the white preoccupation with personal sin and individual separation from God because that emphasis has produced nothing but slavery, segregation, and racial discrimination. In the final analysis, Cone understands sin to manifest itself as follows: an individual disconnects himself from the liberating activity of God, dehumanizes nonwhites, and then ultimately oppresses them. After reading Cone's definition, one is left to wonder if it is possible for blacks to sin at all.

---

[86]Ibid., 104.
[87]Ibid.
[88]Ibid., 105.
[89]Ibid.
[90]Ibid.
[91]Ibid., 107.

BLACK THEOLOGY IS BEYOND BLACK OPPRESSION

According to Cone's theology, there is "no truth in Jesus Christ independent of the oppressed in the land—their history and culture."[92] Again, for Cone any view of the gospel that "fails to see Jesus as liberator of the oppressed is heretical."[93] Furthermore, any view that does not ground ecclesiology in the community of oppressed victims is not Christian and is thus heretical.[94]

According to black theology, Christian theology exists to systematize and categorize God's work to assist oppressed victims in their liberation.[95] Black theology deals with the black experience of oppression but includes all individuals in America who are people of color: black, yellow, red, and brown.[96] The word *black* becomes a metaphor, then, for all those who were or are oppressed in America by "white" people.[97]

> The extermination of Amerindians, the persecution of Jews, the oppression of Mexican-Americans, and every other conceivable inhumanity done in the name of God and country—these brutalities can be analyzed in terms of the white American inability to recognize humanity in persons of color. If the oppressed of this land want to challenge the oppressive character of white society, they must begin affirming their identity in terms of the reality that is anti-white. Blackness, then, stands for all victims of oppression who realize that the survival of their humanity is bound up with liberation from whiteness.[98]

Whiteness, Cone suggests in his early writings, is a symbol of the Antichrist, characterized by the activity of "deranged individuals" consumed by their own image of themselves and consequently unable to see the social injustice in the world.[99]

---

[92]Ibid., 33.
[93]Ibid., 37.
[94]Ibid.
[95]Cone, *A Black Theology of Liberation*, 5.
[96]Cone, *God of the Oppressed*, 33–34.
[97]Cone never defines what *white* is other than to refer back to descendants from Europe. As an unspecified term, *white* will be used to include people of western and eastern European descent. *Black* will include African slaves brought to the Americas during the slave trade as well as modern-day Africans and blacks in developing nations.
[98]Cone, *A Black Theology of Liberation*, 7.
[99]Ibid.

According to Cone, "white theology," which he never defines specifically, is a theology of white oppressors, serving as a divine sanction for criminal acts committed against blacks.[100] Cone does explain that American theologians, from Cotton Mather and Jonathan Edwards to Reinhold Niebuhr and Schubert Odgen, interpret the gospel according to the cultural and political interests of white people, rarely attempting to transcend the issues of their group by seeking an analysis of the gospel in the light of black people's struggle for liberation.[101]

Cone confesses in a similar fashion that a black theology that deals exclusively with oppression is shaped by the cultural and political existence of the victims—i.e., people of color—in North America.[102] European and African immigrants to this country must be distinguished according to each group's legacy of suffering because Europeans came here escaping tyranny, and Africans came "in chains to serve a nation of tyrants."[103] This distinction is important in the indictments that are launched against white theology by black theologians because liberation from oppression is a central theme in black theology.[104] For Cone, God is a political God, the protector of the poor, and the harbinger of justice for those who are oppressed.[105] To know God is to know him as one who liberates the weak and helpless from pain and humiliation.[106]

According to black theology, the Old Testament substantiates the theology of liberation, beginning with the Exodus story. There Yahweh revealed himself as a liberator and savior of an oppressed people. By extension, then, there can be no knowledge of Yahweh "except through his political activity on behalf of the weak and helpless of the land."[107] For Cone, God's choosing an oppressed people to be his people has profound implications for developing

---

[100]Ibid., 9.
[101]Cone, *God of the Oppressed*, 47.
[102]Ibid., 53.
[103]Ibid.
[104]Diana L. Hayes, *And Still We Rise: An Introduction to Black Liberation Theology* (Mahwah, NJ: Paulist Press, 1996), 186–197.
[105]Cone, *God of the Oppressed*, 63.
[106]Ibid.
[107]Ibid.

theology. Israel's election cannot be disconnected from its "servitude and liberation."[108] God chose Israel because they were weak, help-less, and oppressed. God, in the end, "is the God of history whose will is identical with the liberations of the oppressed from social and political bondage."[109]

God's commitment to the poor and oppressed, as demonstrated in the Old Testament, prevents black theology from taking certain sides in politics.[110] To be neutral or to side with the oppressors is to be unbiblical. "If theology does not side with the poor, then it can-not speak for Yahweh, who is the God of the poor," writes Cone.[111] As God's revelation is made known to humanity, it comes primarily in and through the cultural situations of oppressed victims.[112]

In black theology, the New Testament reveals the good news that Jesus Christ came to liberate the poor and oppressed victims and to inaugurate God's kingdom. Because of this, his work in the kingdom is "bound up with his person as disclosed in his identi-fication with the poor."[113] Christ, the suffering servant, exercises his kingship by bringing justice to his people. He has come to take others' pain and affliction upon himself, "thereby redeeming them *from* oppression and *for* freedom."[114] This is the key to Jesus' mis-sion. The absence of understanding the work and person of Christ in terms of oppression and liberation is seen as a key weakness in "white" American theology by black theologians.

> The weakness of white American theology is that it seldom gets beyond the first century in its analysis of revelation. If I read the New Testament correctly, the resurrection of Jesus means that he is present today in the midst of all societies, bringing about the liberation of the oppressed. He is not confined to the first century; thus our talk of him in the past is important only insofar as it leads us to an *encounter* with him *now* . . . the failure of white theology

---

[108]Ibid., 65.
[109]Ibid.
[110]Ibid., 70.
[111]Ibid., 71.
[112]Cone, *A Black Theology of Liberation*, 28.
[113]Cone, *God of the Oppressed*, 74.
[114]Ibid., 75, italics his.

to speak to the black liberation struggle only reveals once again the racist character of white thought.[115]

Jesus refused to separate himself from the poor or from his mission to liberate the poor and oppressed victims. Even Satan himself was unsuccessful in tempting Jesus away from this calling. Cone believes that the temptation narrative in the Gospels "affirms that Jesus rejected such roles as wonder worker or political king, because they would separate him from the suffering of the poor, the very people he had come to liberate."[116]

POST–CONIAN THEOLOGICAL REFLECTIONS ON BLACK CONSCIOUSNESS

Unless there is oppression, Cone said, there is no freedom in God. God's freedom for humanity is liberation from oppression.[117] Cone asserts that "there can be no freedom for God in isolation from the humiliated and abused. There can be no freedom for God unless the hungry are fed, the sick are healed, and justice is given to the poor."[118] It is simply not possible to be free unless one is politically and/or socially oppressed. Anticipating objections, Cone offers these questions:

> Who are the oppressed? What does black theology mean by oppression? Is black theology saying that only black people are oppressed and, further, that oppression is limited to social, political, and economic reality? What about the obvious oppression of others not of African descent and also the oppressors themselves that can be described as mental or spiritual oppression? After all, are we not *all* oppressed, especially those who think that their freedom is found in social, political, and economic domination of others?[119]

In answering these questions, Cone clarifies by saying that when oppressors ask these questions, they are not genuine, as oppressors

---

[115]Cone, *A Black Theology of Liberation*, 30, italics his.
[116]Cone, *God of the Oppressed*, 75.
[117]Ibid., 147.
[118]Ibid.
[119]Ibid., 148.

intend to "play the victim" to maintain dominance. Since the only true Christians are oppressed victims, these questions from the mouths of oppressors have no credibility. To be an oppressor and to ask these questions reveals a desire "to be oppressors and Christians at the same time."[120] The definition of "the oppressed" is described in this way:

> While it is true that all are oppressed (and especially those who rule over others), only those whose existence (and thus conscious-ness) is defined by the liberation of people from social, political, and economic bondage can understand the dialectic of oppression and freedom in the practice of liberation. Therefore, when white theological rulers claim, "We are all oppressed!" they are speaking the truth, although they do not understand the truth. To do so, the truth would have to be reflected in their struggle to free themselves from their culture in order to join the cultural freedom of the poor. Until their consciousness is born anew in the light of black libera-tion, the truth of the statement is limited to verbal propositions that may be interesting for academicians but of little consequence for the freedom of the poor.[121]

In addition, limiting the historical era in which oppression exists seems to be crucial for determining who is oppressed. For example, those who are oppressed during the era of Cone's choosing tend to fall into the category of those in need of liberation theology. Previous historical oppression by those identified as the oppressors or the cycling in and out of oppression seems to matter little, if at all.

Much of this devaluing of time and history is found in Cone's understanding of the origins of truth. For Cone, truth exists not in words but in "the dynamic of the divine-human encounter in social existence wherein people recognize the connections between his-torical struggle and ultimate reality."[122] For oppressed victims, their consciousness is defined by their status as victims of oppression. Cone is quite content with African-American victimology and with using that victimology as a hermeneutic for theology. In the end, the

---

[120]Ibid.
[121]Ibid.
[122]Ibid., 149.

fact that Cone and others treat political oppression as historically and psychologically limiting severely undermines their entire project in the long rum.[123]

Cone does note, however, that history plays a major role in explaining the relationship between liberation and freedom. There is no liberation outside of the context of one's commitment to "revolutionary action against injustice, slavery, and oppression."[124] Cone limits this struggle to two groups: (1) the Israelites in Egypt and (2) black people during the time of American slavery.[125] This limitation is something he regrets in later writings and something for which he is criticized in response to his early writings. Despite these criticisms, Cone later expands his analysis only to third-world countries and to those countries that find themselves victims of "poverty, colonialism, human rights [abuses], and monopoly capitalism" in Africa, Latin America, the Caribbean, and Asia.[126]

In general, whites are still the primary source of black oppression and of the unfortunate low socioeconomic status of some blacks. As late as 1984, Cone still maintained that people of color were, in general, being oppressed by white Americans, Europeans, and South Africans.[127] The oppressors of the world are "white," and the victims of that oppression are people of color everywhere in the world.[128] Political oppression, in Cone's vision, is perpetrated only by white people against all other races and cultures of color. Cone encourages racial groups all over the world to

> band together for the liberation of all. African-Americans cannot gain their freedom in the U.S.A. until peoples throughout the world are set free. It's a common struggle; there will be no freedom for any one of us until all of us are set free. Oppressors know that,

---

[123]James H. Cone and Gayraud S. Wilmore, eds., *Black Theology: A Documentary History, Volume II: 1980–1992* (Maryknoll, NY: Orbis Books, 1993), 1–11.
[124]Cone, *God of the Oppressed*, 152.
[125]Ibid.
[126]Cone, *A Black Theology of Liberation*, xvii.
[127]Cone, *For My People*, 142.
[128]Robert E. Hood, *Begrimed and Black: Christian Traditions on Blacks and Blackness* (Minneapolis: Fortress Press, 1994), 115–180.

and that is why white South Africans and Americans are such good friends, à la Ronald Reagan and Margaret Thatcher.[129]

Cone encourages dialogue and camaraderie, as people all over the world continue to be oppressed by whites.[130] Since North American whites and Europeans are, by default, guilty of oppression world-wide, black theologians in America, having now learned from third-world theologians, analyze racism "in relation to international capitalism, imperialism, colonialism, world poverty, classism, and sexism."[131] There is a perceived connection between black poverty in the United States and third-world poverty with the abuses of white churches in the United States and white missionaries in the third world.[132]

Third-world theologians and black liberation theologians apply their theology out of shared experience in poor ghettoes, villages, and churches in their respective countries.[133] Internationally, the focus of liberation theology is the European invasion of the continents of Africa, Asia, and Latin America, which inaugurated the slave trade as well as colonialism and neocolonialism.[134] The definition of *poor* is expanded by black theologians to include not only oppressed blacks in America but all nonwhite racial groupings who have been oppressed by descendants of Europe all over the world through various means during selected historical periods. Liberation theology, therefore, includes any ethnic group seeking economic and political liberation from "Euro-American domination."[135] Liberation theology in the world at large contains, then, four key methodological components: (1) It engages complex religious-cultural contexts with the political commitment to liberate the poor from oppression; (2) it contains thorough social analysis; (3) it contains a political commitment to reinterpret Scripture in light of the abuses that European and North American theologians

---

[129]Cone, *For My People*, 142.
[130]Ibid.
[131]Ibid., 146.
[132]Ibid., 146–147.
[133]Ibid., 148.
[134]Ibid., 149.
[135]Ibid., 151.

engendered; and (4) it requires that theological concepts be reread from the Bible and adapted by indigenous and native communities in ways not communicated by European and white North American norms.[136]

One question that must be raised, however, is this: how far back should the analysis extend in order to determine who the oppressors are and who comes from a history of an oppressed people? Does there exist anywhere in the world a people at any time in human history that has never oppressed others? When Cone speaks of liberation theology being for those groups that have a historical connection with struggle, how far back in history are we to delve in order to make the case? Moreover, why limit studies of oppression to the western slave trade and colonialism? Why is recent history the only relevant history?

By focusing exclusively on the black experience, black liberation theologians often overlook other groups who were and still are politically oppressed around the world. Internationally, liberation theologians arbitrarily choose certain oppressed groups and overlook others. Historically speaking, however, there is not a people group on earth that has not, at some point, been both the oppressed and the oppressor. If this is true, does Cone's contention that all individuals descend either from oppressed victims or from oppressors become a false dichotomy?

The failure to incorporate world history into the analysis of oppression tends to render black theology ineffective. Using Cone's rationale of limiting oppression to political oppression, the application of liberation will include both North American whites as well as western and eastern Europeans. Black theology formulated after Cone's initial development also fails to recognize interethnic oppression. Oppression among different African tribal groups, among Native American civilizations in North and South America, among Asian civilizations, and so on is completely overlooked and ignored in black liberation theology. Additionally, the oppression

---

[136]Ibid., 151–153.

of Caucasian groups by other Caucasian groups in Europe and the Americas is also ignored.[137]

HEALING THE VICTIMOLOGIST BLACK CONSCIOUSNESS

What is needed to deal with slavery, racism, and structural sin is the application of justice. In black theology, this justice, never defined specifically, is derived primarily through socioeconomic means. For black theology, and the black church in general, the economic status of blacks, from the Reconstruction era forward, has been understood as proportional to the educational and moral development of the black community.[138] There can be no large gains in education and moral development outside of improvement in the overall economic status of blacks.

In response to the historical subjugation of blacks by whites in America, black theologians writing on the topic of social ethics are seeking political, economic, and social power for marginalized blacks.[139] When there is equality of power and resources, justice will have been achieved. Further, Cone writes, "No theme has been more prominent in black religious thought than the justice of God."[140] God's justice is uniquely tied to his liberation of oppressed victims and punishment of the oppressors. Black theologians' belief in the coming justice of God is "the chief reason blacks have been able to hold themselves together in their struggle for freedom, even though the odds are usually against them."[141] In order to separate an understanding of God's love from "white theology," it is important to emphasize the fact that love, in black religious language, is usually linked with God's justice, liberation, and hope.[142] As noted earlier, black theology is adapted to deal with

---

[137]See Thomas Sowell, *Ethnic America* (New York: Basic Books, 1981) and Thomas Sowell, *Conquests and Cultures: An International History* (New York: Basic Books, 1998).

[138]Peter J. Paris, *The Social Teachings of the Black Churches* (Philadelphia: Fortress Press, 1985), 69–70.

[139]J. Deotis Roberts, "A Creative Response to Racism: Black Theology," in *The Church and Racism*, ed. Gregory Baum and John Coleman (New York: Seabury Press, 1982), 39.

[140]James H. Cone, *Speaking the Truth: Ecumenism, Liberation, and Black Theology* (Grand Rapids, MI: Eerdmans, 1986), 84.

[141]Ibid.

[142]Ibid.

black people's struggle for justice in a nation where the social, political, and economic structures are dominated by white racist ideology.

Seeking social justice, according to Cone, is what differentiated the Christian religious expression of black slaves from their white slaveholders. Slaves embraced Christ to affirm their dignity and empower themselves for freedom, whereas whites used their Christian identity to dominate others.[143] While the great majority of white Christian people condoned slavery, says Cone, black slaves believed that God justly willed their freedom from the racism and oppression of whites.[144] Later Martin Luther King Jr. would come as an agent of justice who interpreted God's love in light of "justice for the poor, liberation for all, and the certain hope that God has not left this world in the hands of evil men."[145]

Bruce Fields agrees that the Bible demonstrates God's demand for justice on behalf of the powerless and gives them special attention. However, Fields cautions that "other characteristics of the God of the exodus must be considered; otherwise, the emerging picture of God is one of mere force for change, and relationship with this force degenerates into a social program," which borders on idolatry.[146] Nicholas Cooper-Lewter and Henry Mitchell highlight the idea that black belief finds its greatest connection with western historical theology on the issue of divine justice.

> Blacks seek a more intensive application of social justice, and they believe that the God of justice is literally on the side of the oppressed. This, along with their sufferings caused by injustice, explained their more energetic efforts to bring about equal opportunity. However, an additional motivation comes from the fact that belief in God's justice also confers meaning on their struggle in the interim, keeping them sane in the midst of crushing absurdities. . . . [T]he just God who is no respecter of persons gives none the power to trample the rights of others with impunity.[147]

---

[143]Ibid., 87.
[144]Ibid., 88.
[145]Ibid., 99.
[146]Bruce Fields, *Introducing Black Theology: Three Crucial Questions for the Evangelical Church* (Grand Rapids, MI: Baker Academic, 2001), 88.
[147]Nicholas Cooper-Lewter and Henry H. Mitchell, *Soul Theology: The Heart of American Black Culture* (Nashville: Abingdon Press, 1991), 30.

The justice of God, pursued and transformed in love, must become a priority of the church. J. Deotis Roberts demands that "sinful social structures must be opposed by structures of righteousness if the evils of the system are to be overcome."[148]

Many black theologians believe that a commitment to bringing justice to these structures and systems will foster equality in the church and in society at large. Justice as liberation produces a context in which those who have been oppressed will attain equality with their oppressors and finally be free. In black theology, this liberation includes economic freedom and independence from white people. Cone is concerned that as long as whites finance black organizations, including church-based ones, whites will control those organizations.[149] The black church, in Cone's view, remains the only institution that is free of "white money" and is therefore free to act independently of the "white ruling class."[150] This economic freedom will allow blacks to control the terms of their liberation in the pursuit of justice.

Economic exploitation, which primarily affects the world's people of color, "is a disease that requires the cooperation of all victims if the world is to be transformed."[151] One of the chief concerns of the black church is to wrestle with the "economic stratification" between whites and blacks.[152] By extension, Cornel West remains adamant that the true liberation of blacks will include both political and socioeconomic liberation.[153] The Marxian approach of redistribution, he believes, will serve as the best evidence of the true liberation of oppressed victims, as multinational companies will no longer be in complete control of the means of production. In West's view, capital accumulation in a free-market economy contributes to the "antidemocratic conditions" that often result in oppression.[154] In other words, profits are made at the expense of others.

---

[148]J. Deotis Roberts, *Black Theology in Dialogue* (Philadelphia: Westminster Press, 1987), 83.
[149]Cone, *For My People*, 202.
[150]Ibid.
[151]Cone, *Speaking the Truth*, 154.
[152]Mary Sawyer, *Black Ecumenism: Implementing the Demands of Justice* (Valley Forge, PA: Trinity Press International, 1994), 10–11.
[153]Cornel West, "Black Theology of Liberation as Critique of Capitalist Civilization," in *Black Theology: A Documentary History, Volume II: 1980–1992*, 416.
[154]Ibid., 417.

In Cone's understanding, the church must act to end the inequal-
ities in the international economic order in terms of the "maldistribution of wealth."[155] If 1 percent of the people in the United States
owns 30 percent of the wealth, "it ought to be clear that black
churches cannot simply continue to ignore socialism as an alternative social arrangement."[156] Freedom for black people is achieved
not only when racism ends but also when economic equality is a
reality.[157] Hopkins believes that "poverty will disappear when the
poor share in the abundance of wealth and break the current global
monopolization of the earth's resources, thereby bringing about
democracy in economics."[158]

CONCLUSION

With this introduction to the formative theological categories
introduced by Cone and further developed by others, it is possible
to understand how victimology establishes the interpretive framework for a victimologist anthropology as well as other categories.
When the black person as victim remains the starting point, black
theology, predictably, continues to veer further away from historic
orthodox Christian theology. In the remainder of the book we will
survey how Cone's introduction of a victimology consciousness for
black people serves as the ultimate starting point for understanding
the development of black theology and all aspects of its vision for
the black church in America.

---

[155]James Cone, *My Soul Looks Back* (Maryknoll, NY: Orbis Books, 1986), 129.
[156]Ibid., 129–130.
[157]Ibid., 136.
[158]Hopkins, *Heart and Head*, 179.

4

Victimology in the Marxist Ethics of Black Theology

Obama will strengthen the ability of workers to organize unions. He will fight for passage of the Employee Free Choice Act. Obama . . . will ensure that his labor appointees support workers' rights and will work to ban the permanent replacement of striking workers. Obama . . . will also increase the minimum wage and index it to inflation to ensure it rises every year.

BARACK OBAMA
CAMPAIGN WEBSITE

✝

One of the articles I wrote for Glenn Beck's newsletter discussed on CNN was a conversation about the connection between Jeremiah Wright's theology and Marxist thought.[1] This chapter is a much more detailed explanation of the connection between the two schools of thought. At the outset, it is important to remind readers that the Marxist connection being made here in no way associates black liberation theologians with the murderous views that many Marxist thinkers have had over the years. The association with Marxism is simply to highlight two things: (1) the connection that many black theologians make to Marx directly, and (2) to explain why good intentions can go wrong if they are not wed with sound structural economics in a way that promotes human dignity and the *imago Dei*.

Marxist thought has had a particularly intriguing relationship

---

[1] "Black Liberation Is Marxist Liberation," March 27, 2008; http://www.glennbeck.com/content/articles/article/198/9520/.

with black liberation theologians over the years. Given the racial and economic history of blacks in America, there has been much debate about possible approaches for improving their general economic plight. Black theologians have a particular interest in the economic implications of social ethics, as they are focused on bringing "economic empowerment" to those who have been victimized.[2] Many black theologians, therefore, have enlisted Marxism as a helpful system for quickly improving the socioeconomic condition of blacks, as Marxist thought is predicated on a system of oppressor class versus victim class.[3]

Unlike Latin American liberation theology, black theology has not enjoyed a long, formal relationship with Marxist thought.[4] In general, black theologians have been slow to fully embrace Marxism.[5] However, James Cone and Cornel West have worked diligently to introduce Marxist thought into black theological discourse, even though the interest in Marxist thought in black theology is, in many ways, more practical than ideological. The affinity for Marxist thought in black theology creates substantial anthropological and economic challenges. This chapter, then, seeks to accomplish two things: (1) to demonstrate the insurgence of Marxism into black theology consistent with the victimologist positions of Cone and West, and (2) to reexamine the use of Marxism in black theology as a means of interpreting the black experience as victim.

DISTINCTIONS IN MARXIST ANTHROPOLOGY

Marxism, at its heart, has no ontological anthropology articulated in its tradition. If, however, one's definition of anthropology is reduced to mere economic functionality, then perhaps "Marxist

---

[2]Theodore Walker Jr., *Empower the People: Social Ethics for the African-American Church* (Maryknoll, NY: Orbis Books, 1991), 120.
[3]Theo Witvliet, *The Way of the Black Messiah: The Hermeneutical Challenge of Black Theology as a Theology of Liberation* (Oak Park, IL: Meyer Stone Books, 1987), 30–31.
[4]See Theodore Weber, "Christian Realism, Power, and Peace," in *Theology, Politics, and Peace*, ed. Theodore Runyon (Maryknoll, NY: Orbis Books, 1989), 71; J. David Turner, *An Introduction to Liberation Theology* (Lanham, MD: University Press of America, 1994), 17–39; and Gustavo Gutierrez, *Essential Writings*, ed. James B. Nickoloff (Maryknoll, NY: Orbis Books, 1996), 45–47.
[5]Patrick Bascio, *The Failure of White Theology: A Black Theological Approach* (New York: Peter Lang, 1994), 33.

anthropology" begins to be somewhat describable because anthropology simply becomes the study of how human beings function the most productively.

Marxism's absence of anthropology as such is due to this fundamental presupposition: human beings have no inherent nature. For the sake of clarity, this aspect of Marxism should be contrasted with Lockean anthropology. John Locke's famous conception of the *tabula rasa* was predicated on the idea that existence precedes essence—viz., one is what one does. While there are patterns of this concept in Marxism, Marx's view of humanity is articulated less clearly but is more broadly based in sociobiology. Marxism views man not as an individual but rather as a species. Alexeiev points out, "Early Marxism regarded man, not as an isolated individual but as 'man in society,' as primary."[6] In this way Marxism is willing to give up the notion of a "person" in exchange for the community. To use a metaphor, pixels do not exist; only the screen.[7]

Overall, Marxism is centrally concerned with social ethics (broadly defined) in such a way that ontological and epistemological categories often go uncategorized. Categories such as action, dynamics, change, and movement take absolute priority over concepts such as being, nature, status, and essence. Therefore, what is called "Marxist anthropology" is really closer to a naturalistic cosmology.[8] Alexeiev goes on to say:

> For Marxism, the nature of man is in the first place conditioned by human interrelations and by man's place in society, the essence of the latter relationship being not that of existing social norms, because such forms are themselves contradictory and are responsible for the "divided," "estranged" nature of man.[9]

Alexeiev uses terms such as "nature" and "essence" in order to make room for Marxist anthropology. And this anthropology, he

---

[6] N. Alexeiev, et al., *The Christian Understanding of Man* (London: George Allen & Unwin Ltd., 1938), 89.
[7] Eugene Kamenka, *Marxism and Ethics* (London: Macmillan and Co. Ltd., 1969), 14. Also Alexeiev, *The Christian Understanding of Man*, 114.
[8] Alexeiev, *The Christian Understanding of Man*, 91.
[9] Ibid., 93.

states, is based on interrelations—that is, man is "social" above all else. Alexeiev is clearer in the following: "Man, according to [Marxist] philosophy, has no personal centre of his own: he is only one of a number of relations for that to which man is related to society, which is not personal (as God is personal) but only a sum-total of relations."[10]

Marxism reduces the classical definitions of what a person is by reducing a "person" to a type of pragmatism. Nothing in oneself denotes "personhood"; the individual is merely a means to another end, the end being the community needs. In the end, as Alexeiev reveals, all that remain are the interactions. An individual, then, has no identity without another. And with another, there are no individuals but only associations.

This pragmatic aspect of Marxism can be seen not only in the Marxist view of human beings but in the Marxist view of anthropology. Hannah Middleton, a Marxist anthropologist, discusses the methodology of anthropology from a distinctly Marxist perspective. In developing a Marxist anthropology, Middleton states, "We start from concrete data on how the people of a particular society, at a particular point in time, associate in order to produce their material means of life."[11] Key ideas such as association and production are axioms of Marxist thought and clearly present in its anthropology.

Here we see the economic aspect of humanity in Marxist thought. Inherent in the ideal nature of human beings is productivity for the sake of the community. Marx himself implies that humanity will not be free to be truly human until liberated from the bondage of laziness and individualism. "Only when the real, individual man . . . as an individual human being has become a species-being [i.e., social] in his everyday life, in his particular work, and in his particular situation . . . only then will human emancipation have been accomplished."[12] Marx ties together productivity and community

---

[10]Ibid., 131.
[11]Hannah Middleton, "Marxist Anthropology," *Australian Marxist Review*, 42 (November 2000).
[12]Klaus Bockmuehl, *The Challenge of Marxism: A Christian Response* (Downers Grove, IL: InterVarsity Press, 1980), 128.

and insists that unless humans have embraced both, they can't have anything like individual credentials; but even those credentials are for the group.

The pragmatism that characterizes a human being is echoed in the historical aspect of humanity. Were a Marxist writing history consistent with his philosophy, he would pay little attention to the contributions of individuals contrasted and isolated from others. Rather, he would recount the successes and failures of the group in its labor and growth as a society, referring to characters only insofar as they did or did not contribute effectively to the social goals. The individuals who make up the community are utterly insignificant.

> For Marxism, therefore, man is a kind of "sandwich-man": for as an individual personality he disappears between the sandwich-boards on which history has inscribed its legend and which he is destined to carry about with him. He has significance in so far as what is written on him is historically good (i.e. progressive).[13]

Alexeiev asserts that Marxism does not believe in the validity of certain ideal values, of personality or the ethic of value, of the categorical imperative, or of moral autonomy as established by the Kantians.[14] The individual, then, does not only function as a means to an end but must also view himself as such. The process of traditional ethics, which calls for each individual to make his own ethical choices, becomes obsolete. Marxism radically erases the individuality of the person, even to such an extent that acting in history with the potential to be productive or unproductive, the person must bow his will completely to the community and its objectives.

Viewing the world exclusively through the lens of social structures sets the stage for Marx's own categories of bourgeois and proletariat as the main distinctions in human community. Moreover, the bourgeois victimize the proletariat economically, and they define social struggle in human history.[15] This view of ethics as a struggle between economic classes was popularized and emerged in

---

[13]Alexeiev, *The Christian Understanding of Man*, 104.
[14]Ibid., 105.
[15]Karl Marx, *The Communist Manifesto* (Chicago, IL: Gateway Editions, 1987), 13ff.

the twentieth-century liberal theology that shaped the thought of James Cone. Reinhold Niebuhr found Marxism useful, with some limits, in his own thinking about social ethics in terms of grouping people by their social location within social classes.[16] Marxism also influenced Jürgen Moltmann, who later incorporated many Marxist themes into his theology of hope.[17] In the process of developing a black liberation theology, Cone drew heavily on the work of Moltmann and even concluded that Moltmann, "who places the Marxist emphasis on action and change," presents a vision of hope that is "compatible with the concerns of black theology."[18] In a natural transition, Cone initiates the incorporation of Marxist ideology into the social ethics of black liberation theology, which continue to be embraced by black liberation theologians such as Cornel West and Dwight Hopkins.

CONE AND MARXISM

In Cone's view, Marxism best addresses remedies to the condition of blacks as victims of white oppression. Cone explains that "the Christian faith does not possess in its nature the means for analyzing the structure of capitalism. Marxism as a tool of social analysis can disclose the gap between appearance and reality, and thereby help Christians to see how things really are."[19] Cone believes that Marx's chief contribution is "his disclosure of the ideological character of bourgeois thought, indicating the connections between the 'ruling *material* force of society' and the 'ruling *intellectual*' force."[20] In this framework, intellectual ideas emerge out of a definitive context—and a socially constructed point of view. Cone praises Marx for noting that truth is a question "not only of what is but of what ought to be."[21] The definition of reality, writes Cone,

---

[16]Stanley J. Grenz and Roger E. Olson, *20th-Century Theology: God and the World in a Transitional Age* (Downers Grove, IL: InterVarsity Press, 1992), 102–106.
[17]Ibid., 173.
[18]James H. Cone, *A Black Theology of Liberation* (Maryknoll, NY: Orbis Books, 1990), 139–140.
[19]James H. Cone, *For My People: Black Theology and the Black Church* (Maryknoll, NY: Orbis Books, 1984), 187.
[20]James H. Cone, *God of the Oppressed* (San Francisco: Harper Collins, 1975), 41, italics his.
[21]Ibid., 42.

is determined by the "existing societal relations of material production, with the ruling class controlling the means of production
as well as the intellectual forces which justify the present political
arrangements."[22] In Marxism, the "oughts" of human community
are defined by what can be accomplished through the "revolutionary praxis of the proletarian class, overthrowing unjust societal
conditions."[23] Marx's thought is useful and attractive to Cone
because it allows black theologians to critique racism in America
on the basis of power and revolution.[24]

Marxists believe that the ruling class's promotion of religion
reveals a conspiracy to sanction materialism and jade the proletariat, leaving them content with humiliation, suffering, and their
own victimization. With this in mind, Cone raises several important
questions that theologians must ask in light of Marx's truth. For
example, "What is the connection between dominant material relations and the ruling theological ideas in a given society?"[25] Taking
Marx seriously, remarks Cone, will make theologians "confess their
limitations, their inability to say anything about God which is not
at the same time a statement about the social context of their own
existence."[26]

According to Cone, theologians must use sources other than
Scripture because there is no objectivity in theology. Although the
revelation of God may be universal, "theological talk about that
revelation is filtered through human experience, which is limited
by their social realities."[27] For Cone, integrating Marx into black
theology helps theologians see just how much social perceptions
determine theological questions and conclusions. Moreover, these
questions and answers are "largely a reflection of the material
condition of a given society."[28] Theologians, in the end, must face

---

[22]Ibid.
[23]Ibid.
[24]African liberation theologians also find Marxism to be a useful tool in evaluating the history
of racism and colonialism. See Itumeleng J. Mosala and Buti Tlhagale, eds., *The Unquestionable
Right to Be Free: Black Theology in South Africa* (Maryknoll, NY: Orbis Books, 1986), 29.
[25]Cone, *God of the Oppressed*, 42.
[26]Ibid., 43.
[27]Ibid.
[28]Ibid.

the fact that their enterprise is merely a reflection of social conditioning. Because of this, neither white nor black theology can avoid the interplay between theology and society. Cone summarizes his reflections on Marx by noting that "what people think about God, Jesus Christ, and the Church cannot be separated from their own social and political status in a given society."[29] Again, it is the self-sufficiency of the black experience as victim that legitimates and calls for a Marxist ethical framework.

It is victimology that drives the paradigm for black theology. Cone appeals to the autonomy of the black experience, using past oppression to brand identity and foster an unfocused resentment and sense of alienation from the mainstream.[30] This explains why black theology must be a theology of liberation.

Cone suggests using different theological categories to understand the nature of God in an effort to throw off the distinctions that were developed apart from the black experience as victim.[31] Cone, however, is careful to reject the atheism of Marxism by disagreeing with those blacks who have accepted a Marxist understanding of the role and function of religion "without probing deeper into the thought forms of black people."[32] For slaves who first heard the gospel on plantations owned and operated by white Christians, it was precisely the work and person of Christ presented in the preaching and teaching of the Scriptures that provided "a knowledge of themselves."[33] It follows, then, that Jesus is confirmed by God in his "blackness" to bring good news to liberate the oppressed, in complete contradiction to Marx's observation regarding the oppressive dimensions of religion.[34]

Cone seeks to go beyond Marx, noting that while Marx is helpful, the problem of oppression is "much more complex" than he envisioned.[35] Cone firmly believes that an analysis that "fails to

---

[29]Ibid., 45.
[30]John H. McWhorter, *Losing the Race: Self-Sabotage in Black America* (New York: Perennial, 2001), 2.
[31]Cone, *God of the Oppressed*, 124.
[32]Ibid., 130.
[33]Ibid.
[34]Ibid., 136.
[35]Ibid., 156.

deal with racism, that demon embedded in white folks' being, is inadequate."[36] American theologians would have written differently, Cone asserts, if Scripture had been interpreted through the eyes of the victimized oppressed rather than through the eyes of white privilege.

CORNEL WEST AND MARXISM

In 1979, Cornel West offered a critical integration of Marxism and black theology in his essay "Black Theology and Marxist Thought," focusing on the shared human experience of oppressed peoples as victims.[37] West sees a strong correlation between black theology and Marxist thought because "both focus on the plight of the exploited, oppressed and degraded peoples of the world, their relative powerlessness and possible empowerment."[38] This common focus prompts West to call for "a serious dialogue between black theologians and Marxist thinkers"—a dialogue that centers on the possibility of "mutually arrived-at political action."[39]

Like Cone, West does not see Christianity as a sufficient source of knowing absolute or objective truth. He writes:

> [T]o believe that truth is an attribute attached exclusively to religious descriptions which promote certain insights and capacities for living is to give way to an expedient existentialism . . . [T]o believe that there is a transcendental standard—a theory-neutral, portrayal-independent, description-free criterion—which enables us to choose true theory portrayal and description is to resign to an Archimedean objectivism.[40]

Employing a Marxist critique, there is no such concept as objective truth, only "specific ever-evolving scientific theories, artistic portrayals, and religious descriptions put forward by particular

---

[36]Ibid.
[37]Cornel West, "Black Theology and Marxist Thought," in *Black Theology: A Documentary History, Volume I: 1966–1979*, ed. James H. Cone and Gayraud S. Wilmore (Maryknoll, NY: Orbis Books, 1979), 552–567.
[38]Ibid., 552.
[39]Ibid.
[40]Cornel West, *Prophesy Deliverance!: An Afro-American Revolutionary Christianity* (Philadelphia: Westminster Press, 1982), 97.

persons, groups, communities, and traditions."[41] As a result, all Christian understandings of the human person and ethics "bear the stamp of their interpreters, the social and personal problems they faced," and the solutions specific to their experiences.[42] West remains cautious that Marxism is plagued with these same limitations, even though it remains a useful tool for black religion.[43]

West argues for a synthesis of black theology and Marxist thought on the following grounds:

> (1) Both adhere to a similar methodology, the same way of approaching their respective subject and arriving at conclusions. (2) Both link some notion of liberation to the future socioeconomic conditions of the downtrodden. (3) And, this is most important, both attempt to put forward trenchant critiques of liberal capitalist America.[44]

West believes that by working together, Marxists and black theologians can spearhead much-needed social change for those who are victims of oppression. He appreciates Marxism for its "notions of class struggle, social contradictions, historical specificity, and dialectical developments in history" that explain the role of power and wealth in bourgeois capitalist societies.[45] A common perspective among Marxist thinkers is that bourgeois capitalism creates and perpetuates ruling-class domination—which for black theologians in America means the domination and victimization of blacks by whites.[46] This Marxist focus supplements a weakness in black theology: focusing too much on the failings of "white North American theology, especially its silence on racial justice and the white racism within mainstream establishment churches and religious agencies."[47]

To put forward a more radical black theology, black theologians

---

[41]Ibid., 97.
[42]Ibid.
[43]Ibid., 100.
[44]West, "Black Theology and Marxist Thought," 553.
[45]West, *Prophesy Deliverance!*, 100.
[46]Claudio J. Katz, *From Feudalism to Capitalism: Marxian Theories of Class Struggle and Social Change* (New York: Greenwood Press, 1989), 38–39.
[47]West, *Prophesy Deliverance!*, 104.

must become more grounded in "the progressive Marxist tradition, with its staunch anti-capitalist, anti-imperialist, anti-racist, and anti-sexist stance and its creative socialist outlook."[48] One of the weaknesses of black theology, from West's perspective, is that it fails to describe what liberation would mean in the everyday lives of black people, what power blacks would possess, and to which resources they would have greater access.[49]

West finds the dialectical methodology of the Hegelian school most appealing and useful for writing social analysis and black theology through the microscope of victimization. For black theologians, a dialectical approach resists uncritical acceptance of dogmatic viewpoints of the gospel by "questioning whether certain unjustifiable prejudgments are operative."[50] Black theology unearths assumptions of particular interpretations of Christianity by "refus[ing] to accept what has been given to them by White theologians."[51] Black theologians know that all reflection about God by whites must be "digested, decoded and deciphered"[52] by black theologians themselves. Using an approach based on sociology of knowledge, black theology preserves the biblical truth "that God sides with the oppressed and acts on their behalf."[53] Marxist social theory takes the bourgeois to task for perpetuating falsehoods about the inhumanity of capitalism; likewise, black theology is critical of "perspectives presented by bourgeois social scientists, questioning whether certain ideological biases are operative."[54]

With these similarities, West calls for more cooperative work between black theologians and Marxists in dealing with black victimology. Because Marxism in general fails to use broader source material, it is overlooked by black theologians as a useful tool for enhancing theological reflection of the black experi-

---

[48]Ibid., 106.
[49]Ibid., 110.
[50]West, "Black Theology and Marxist Thought," 554.
[51]Ibid., 554.
[52]Ibid.
[53]Ibid.
[54]Ibid., 555.

ence as victimized by the white, ruling classes. Additionally, West laments that the lack of Marxist methodology in black theology handicaps black theologians because they cannot "talk specifically about the way in which the existing systems of production and social structure relates to black oppression and exploitation."[55] According to West, black theologians should focus more intently on the unequal distribution of wealth promulgated by the "capitalist system of production."[56] West cites James Cone as the only voice in black theology who reflected on the intersection of black theology and economics concerning black victims' structural oppression. Later West actually chided black theologians for adopting bourgeois ideologies through their embracing capitalism. These theologians, West believes, should trade in their commitment to liberation for a commitment to "inclusion."[57] In this sense, many black theologians have simply become a part of the problem.

From a Marxist perspective, social liberation occurs only when blacks are able to participate substantially in the decision-making processes of the major institutions that regulate their lives as victims. West complains:

> Black theologians hardly mention the wealth, power, and influence of multinational corporations that monopolize production in the marketplace and prosper, partially owing to their dependence on public support in the form of government subsidies, free technological equipment, lucrative contacts and sometimes even direct-transfer payments.[58]

Embracing West's challenge, black theologian Dwight Hopkins offers the following analysis regarding multinationals and people of color around the world:

> Further intricate unfoldings of the cultural revelation of the religion of globalization appear with the McDonaldization of the

---

[55]Ibid.
[56]Ibid.
[57]Ibid.
[58]Ibid., 557. See also West, *Prophesy Deliverance!*, 113–114.

world, closely pursued by KFC and Burger King. What these fast food monopoly capitalist corporations have in common with Pepsi and Coca Cola is the refined art of creating and altering the food tastes of the indigenous populations in developing countries. They effect a smooth strategy. U.S. soft drink monopolies undercut prices of locally brewed soda pop, purchase a monopoly on the coin soda dispensing machines in a country, and flood the market with massive advertising linking their product with youth, sex, sports, and happy faces.[59]

In theory, having positions of power in these areas will ensure that blacks all over the world will be treated equally and will not succumb to regression into victimhood.

Unlike Cone, however, West views class as being more a determiner of powerlessness than race. Only class divisions, West explains, define who is rich and who is poor as well as why some groups experience more luxuries than others do. According to West, class divisions, defined by the unequal distribution of goods and services, provide the platform to foster "racism, sexism, and ageism."[60] West maintains that "significant degrees of powerlessness pertain to most Americans, and this could be so only if class position determines such powerlessness. Therefore, class position contributes more than racial status to the basic form of powerlessness in America."[61] For example, the black middle class no longer living near poor blacks has left poor blacks even more vulnerable to being taken advantage of by whites.[62]

West is careful to note that a class analysis in liberation theologies does not bring with it a natural affinity between black and Latin American liberation theologies. Latin American theologians typically belong to the dominant power group in their respective

---

[59]Dwight N. Hopkins, *Heart and Head: Black Theology—Past, Present, and Future* (New York: Palgrave, 2002), 151–152.
[60]West, "Black Theology and Marxist Thought," 560.
[61]West, *Prophesy Deliverance!*, 115.
[62]Stephen Breck Reid, "The Theology of the Book of Daniel and the Political Theory of W.E.B. DuBois," in *The Recovery of Black Presence: An Interdisciplinary Exploration: Essays In Honor of Dr. Charles B. Copher*, ed. Randall C. Bailey and Jacquelyn Grant (Nashville: Abingdon Press, 1995), 48. Also see William Julius Wilson, *When Work Disappears: The World of the New Urban Poor* (New York: Alfred A. Knopf, 1996), 25–110 and Allan Aubrey Boesak, *Black Theology, Black Power* (London: Mowbrays, 1978), 100.

countries. Furthermore, these theologians, "educated in either European schools or Europeanized Latin American universities and seminaries . . . adopt cosmopolitan habits and outlooks" like their bourgeois "master," Karl Marx.[63] Latin American liberation theologians do not emerge from a position of social oppression.[64]

West concludes that one of the main obstacles to the full embrace of Marxism by black theology is the dominance in black thought of a certain Leninism.[65] The Leninist stream reeks of the rigidity, dogmatism, and elitism characteristic of the very ruling class that Leninists oppose.[66] For West, Leninism is to Marxism what conservative evangelicalism is to Christianity: "orthodox and fundamentalist outlooks which give self-serving lip service to truncated versions of the major norms."[67] It is the Leninist, right-wing Marxism that keeps black theologians from fully using Marx in their theology. In the end, a true, revolutionary, progressive, Marxist black liberation program has many political goals including, on the one hand, to *"weaken the hegemony of liberalism over the Afro-American community (especially its leadership) and to break the stronghold of Leninism over Afro-American Marxists."*[68] By extension, a revolutionary Christian perspective for the black community must

> remain anchored in the prophetic Christian tradition in the Afro-American experience, which provides the norms of individuality and democracy; guided by the cultural outlook of the Afro-American humanist tradition, which promotes the vitality and vigor of black life; and informed by the social theory and political praxis of progressive Marxism, which proposes to appropriate as close as possible the precious values of individuality and democracy as soon as God's will be done.[69]

---

[63]West, "Black Theology and Marxist Thought," 561.
[64]Ibid., 561. See also West, *Prophesy Deliverance!*, 117–118. See George C. L. Cummings, *A Common Journey: Black Theology (USA) and Latin American Liberation Theology* (Maryknoll, NY: Orbis Books, 1993), 90–98.
[65]West, *Prophesy Deliverance!*, 138. Earlier West describes six streams of Marxist thought: the Bernsteinian, Leninist, Stalinist, Trotskyist, Councilist, and Gramscian streams (134).
[66]Ibid., 136.
[67]Ibid., 137.
[68]Ibid., 140, italics his.
[69]Ibid., 146.

POINTS OF DEPARTURE FROM MARXISM WITHIN BLACK THEOLOGY

After some initial engagement with Marxist thinkers, many black theologians have expressed reservations about its use. Nearly ten years after Cone promoted a closer relationship with Marxist thinkers, he discovered that white Marxists were no less condescending and racist than anyone else.[70] Moreover, black theologians who adopted the Marxist class analysis did nothing more than justify the interests of middle-class blacks. Cone recalls, "[A]lthough claiming to speak for the poor, we actually spoke for ourselves."[71]

Additionally, the arrogance of white socialists in previous encounters within the academic community became a stumbling block for black theologians. Cone states, "[T]he arrogant attitude of white socialists is one of the reasons why socialism is a 'foreign' word in the black community. . . . [T]he continued presence of racism among socialists is evidence enough that socialism alone will not solve the racial problems in the world."[72]

Cone resents white Marxists because they have controlled the language of Marxist incorporations into Christian theology and think that their view of the gospel and Marxism vetoes all other perspectives. "When [whites] urged minorities to transcend their particularities and embrace Marxism, they mean *European* Marxism—as interpreted by *them*," says Cone.[73]

Other Christian intellectuals, in addition to Cone, have reservations about the use of Marxism. Moellering believes that Marxism serves as a secularizing force in Christianity.[74] Some black theologians believe that Cone's use of Marxism will actually isolate the black church from the rest of Christendom.[75] While an unbridled Marxism is too restrictive for some black liberation theologians

---

[70]Cone, *For My People*, 29.
[71]Ibid., 94–95.
[72]Ibid., 171.
[73]Ibid., 173, italics his.
[74]Ralph L. Moellering, "Marxism and the Secular," in *Christian Hope and the Secular*, ed. Daniel F. Martensen (Minneapolis: Augsburg, 1969), 82–91.
[75]See the comments of J. H. Jackson, former president of the National Baptist Convention, the largest African-American denomination in the United States, in Noel Leo Erskine, *King among Theologians* (Cleveland: Pilgrim Press, 1994), 94.

because of the atheism, one black theologian does praise the system for uplifting the "general economic welfare of the group."[76] Black liberation theologian J. Deotis Roberts flatly rejects the use of Marxism, contending that it is "godlessness" in powerful form and leads to great evil and suffering.[77]

However, even with these reservations, Cone remains committed to Marxism as a needed system for applying the gospel in the black community and protecting the black church from white theology and white oppression. Cone sees the rejection of Marxism by some black theologians as unfortunate, due to an affinity to the anti-Communist attitude of the white church. Cone writes, "[C]onservative white Christians associate capitalism with Christian freedom and political democracy, and they identify Marxism with Russian communism, atheism, and political totalitarianism."[78] Cone blames the failures in Vietnam, the abysmal "war on poverty," and the violent revolutionary tactics in the socialist third world for preventing blacks from taking Marxism seriously.[79]

Marxism helps the black church discern how white Christians used religion as an opiate during slavery and reconstruction. The practice of Christianity by white Christians in the past—and even in recent times—gives credence to Marx's claim about the role of religion when used by the oppressor. Cone notes:

> Almost without exception, white American churches have interpreted religion as something exclusively spiritual with no political content useful in the struggles of the poor for freedom. By identifying the gospel of Jesus with a spirituality estranged from the struggle for justice, the church becomes an agent of injustice. . . . [U]nfortunately, all institutional white churches in America have sided with capitalist, rich, white, male elites, and against socialists, the poor, blacks, and women.[80]

---

[76]Dwight N. Hopkins, *Down, Up, and Over: Slave Religion and Black Theology* (Minneapolis: Fortress Press, 2000), 251.

[77]J. Deotis Roberts, *Black Religion, Black Theology: The Collected Essays of J. Deotis Roberts* (Harrisburg, PA: Trinity Press International, 2003), 173. See P. Morris, "Judaism and Capitalism," in *Religion and the Transformation of Capitalism: Comparative Approaches,* ed. Richard H. Roberts (London: Routledge, 1995), 88–90.

[78]Cone, *For My People*, 176.

[79]Ibid., 178.

[80]Ibid., 182.

In fact, one black theologian believes that "American monopoly capitalism engenders white supremacy" and that capitalism as a system, therefore, needs to be abolished.[81] This conclusion logically follows the belief that capitalism tends toward the control of the poor, especially if the poor, in the eyes of some, are black.[82]

THE THEORETICAL LIMITS OF A VICTIMOLOGIST APPROACH TO MARXISM

In his work on Marxist ways of thinking, social and economic theorist Thomas Sowell, as an African-American contemporary of Cone and West, gives the most cogent analysis of the use of Marxism to address victimologists' presuppositions in black religious and social thought.[83] Thomas Sowell warns against both quick allegiance to—and unexamined rejection of—the philosophy and economics of Karl Marx and the Marxist school of thought when confronting strained economic environments presupposing victimology. Because Marx wrote against specific competing doctrines of his day, many of which, says Sowell, "have disappeared into obscurity, so later interpreters have not fully understood what it was that Marx and Engels were arguing against," black liberation theologians should be wary of applying Marxist doctrine to black experience.[84] In fact, what often emerges in black theology is a Marxism that may be unrelated to what Marx actually intended.

Like Cone, Sowell highlights the Hegelian dialectical approach used by Marx. However, there continues to be debate regarding the extent to which Marx fully incorporates Hegel's dialectical approach.[85] Marxists look for patterns, distinguishing between the

---

[81]See Dwight N. Hopkins, *Shoes That Fit Our Feet: Sources for a Constructive Black Theology* (Maryknoll, NY: Orbis Books, 1993), 186.

[82]Tamar Diana Wilson, "Theoretical Approaches to the Informal Sector," in *Development in Theory and Practice: Latin American Perspectives,* ed. Ronald H. Chilcote (Lanham, MD: Rowman and Littlefield, 2003), 113.

[83]Thomas Sowell, *Marxism: Philosophy and Economics* (New York: Quill, 1985) and Thomas Sowell, *Knowledge and Decisions* (New York: Basic Books, 1986). I depend heavily here on Sowell as a conversation partner with Cone and West and as contemporaries with the most codified alternative perspectives on victimology in black social thought.

[84]Sowell, *Marxism,* 177–178.

[85]For a good discussion of Marx's use of Hegel, see Tony Smith, *Dialectical Social Theory and Its Critics: From Hegel to Analytical Marxism and Postmodernism* (Albany, NY: State University of New York Press, 1993), 35–47.

inner essence and the outer appearance, an approach that rejects all uncritical acceptance of ideas, doctrines, and the like, seeking instead "the inner pattern from which these appearances derive and evolve."[86] For example, Cone, employing a Marxist methodology, looks for patterns of racist thought and black victimology to conclude that white American theology has no interest in addressing the needs of blacks. For Cone, white theology is simply patterned this way, rendering blacks as victims of wanton neglect.

Marx's work is driven by a tendency toward "abstraction, systematic analysis, and successive approximations to a reality too complex to grasp directly."[87] As a result, Marx often uses broad generalizations, many times unsubstantiated, to establish the identity of those he defines as victims. This pattern, adopted by black theologians such as Cornel West, James Cone, Dwight Hopkins, and others, produces broad generalizations that often take the form of describing the whole of the black experience in America as one of being victimized by white oppression.

Sowell points out that "historical justification" is the "only justification—the supreme ethical principle" for Marx.[88] Namely, this is the idea that justice is discerned according to the demand of a certain historical context—the autonomous experience of a collection of individuals. In one context, according to Marx, certain practices may be permissible, while in another they would be unethical. For example, certain forms of slavery and oppression were considered to be justified at various stages in history.[89] One wonders if Cone was actually aware that a key presupposition of Marx's thought justified the type of oppression considered anathema to Cone and to other black liberation theologians. Marx did, however, believe that just because a certain system could be justified in the past did not mean that it should remain so in the present or in the future. Slavery, once it became economically questionable, for example, could be justifiably abolished.

---

[86]Sowell, *Marxism*, 18.

[87]Ibid.

[88]Ibid., 23

[89]Ibid. See also R. G. Peffer, *Marxism, Morality, and Social Justice* (Princeton, NJ: Princeton University Press, 1990), 334–336.

Marx's confession that slavery is at times justified raises questions about how much of Marx's writings Cone actually surveyed before deciding to laud him as a model thinker for the black church. If Cone rejects Jonathan Edwards for owning slaves, Cone should also reject Marx, based on his allowance for slavery under certain conditions. If white intellectuals who promote slavery under certain circumstances are anathema to Cone, why is Marx given a platform to direct the social analysis of black theology?

The concept of an autonomous, self-sufficient personal "development" is central to Marx's thought and thus fits seamlessly with the position of autonomous black experience promoted by black liberation theologians. Marx asserts that full humanity is actualized through one's own "productive work."[90] As a result, when the human person is not able to develop in his work, he is oppressed—he is a victim. For example, according to Marx, the assembly-line worker under capitalism is oppressed because the repetition of that work reduces him to an "it" instead of a person.[91] Black liberation theologians such as Cone and West adopt this idea by objecting to the way in which the capitalist "means of production" controls the poor and limits their freedom, thus oppressing them. Marx also believes that in a capitalist system, people are alienated from their humanity and become subject to the means of production instead of employing those means. West concurs, commenting that it is capitalism that controls people instead of people controlling capitalism.[92] People are not free to develop as they choose because capitalism imprisons workers.

MARXIST EQUIVOCATIONS IN BLACK THEOLOGY: AN ANALYSIS

Theoretically speaking, Cone, West, and others wrongly see the conflict between management and labor as one of control and power. The limited freedom that Marx speaks about, however, is different

---

[90]Ibid., 25.
[91]Ibid., 26.
[92]See Anthony Giddens, *Capitalism and Modern Social Theory: An Analysis of the Writings of Marx, Durkheim, and Max Weber* (Cambridge: Cambridge University Press, 1971), 35–36.

from the limited freedom that Cone speaks of, even though the language is the same. For Marx, people are alienated because their work may at times be monotonous, whereas for Cone, alienation is broadly applied to power, control, and social alienation. Marx, therefore, concludes that those who control the means of production control the laborers; however, this point, misunderstood by black theologians, is wrongly applied to the black experience in America. What black theologians want is black control of the means of production—something that Marx would have rejected in principle. The race of the ones in control of production is not the issue in a true Marxist framework as much as is the workers' ability to do different types of jobs. Many black theologians, however, are primarily concerned only with the race element. If blacks controlled the means of production, thus alienating whites, this action, in the black liberation framework, would be justifiable and thus permissible—as long as blacks are in control.

Marx's theory of history, adopted by Cone in his theological analysis, maintains that "men are products of their environments in general, and of their economic environment in particular."[93] Cone uses this approach to explain how white theology is a product not of biblical exegesis but of white economic and political power structures that continue to oppress and historically victimized people of color.

Black theologians also misunderstand Marx in his understanding of causation. Black liberation theologians tend to rely on economic explanations to evaluate culture in a certain way. However, writes Sowell,

> the Marxian theory of history did not attempt to explain the law and politics of a given era as deriving solely from the economic relations of that era. That would be explaining isolated states of being as if each era were hermetically sealed and began from nothing, rather than from the preceding era. What Marxian theory attempted to explain were the changes from one era to another—the social transformations of "development" in dialectical terms.[94]

---

[93]Sowell, *Marxism*, 53.
[94]Ibid., 57.

Moreover, in true Marxist theory, it is not permissible to present a list of methodologies and propositions abstracted from the problems they are supposed to illuminate.[95] Therefore, using the current plight of blacks to elucidate prescriptions against white Christians and white churches is a misapplication of Marxist social theory.

According to Sowell, Marx is careful not to conjecture that economic interests determine ideas. Sowell contends, "Marx saw a logic in the pattern of historical events, but did not impute this logic to the agents involved in these events, or to those who bring about historical transformations. Marx cautioned that 'we must not form the narrow-minded notion that the petty bourgeoisie, on principle, wishes to enforce an egoist class interest.'"[96] This notion, however, is exactly what Cone and West conclude in their critique of white theology. A false understanding of Marx in this sense would lead us to believe that he would disapprove of attempts to define a white motive to control blacks. For Marx, class self-interest is not so much a shaper of ideas, but rather "'the economic relations— that is, the human relations growing out of production—shape the conflicting perceptions that lead to historic struggles and social transformations.'"[97] Economics explain, in a limited sense, how things have changed, but it may not explain why. For Marx, it is the source of change, rather than the weight of change, that matters the most in seeking social improvements.[98] While using economics might be useful to black theologians in explaining what changes have occurred from one era to the next, it does not explain the whole of what white churches did or did not do in relation to certain social realities.

In Marxist thought, the conflict between classes is difficult to narrowly explain. Sowell states, "If there is no subjective sense of solidarity and no ideological principle or behavior pattern peculiar to [a] group as classified . . . the classification is arbitrary and

---

[95]Michael Harrington, *The Twilight of Capitalism* (New York: Simon and Schuster, 1976), 190.
[96]Sowell, *Marxism*, 60–61.
[97]Ibid., 61.
[98]Ibid., 64.

barren."[99] In other words, social groups that acquire no common ideologies—or no cohesive organization with which to promote their ideologies—are not truly classes, in the Marxian sense. Therefore speaking of "blacks" or "the poor" as distinct victimized and oppressed classes is plausible only if these groups have common ideologies and are not competing against each other.[100] Because of the differences, then, in the black theological community, as evidenced in black theology texts, it is impossible to speak broadly about "white American theology" or even "black theology" as distinct theological classes.[101] Additionally, speaking about black and whites too broadly creates similar problems that Marxism intended to remedy.

Just as it is inaccurate to broadly use the term *white* to describe a class—economic or otherwise—there is a sense in which Marx might reject Cone's use of the term *black* to describe his project as well. The components that make a class a class or a group a group, in Marx's view, challenge Cone's ability to make a case for certain prescriptions made for all black Americans. In other words, this aspect of Marx's thinking renders Cone and other black theologians powerless in making arguments for or about black people as a whole. Blacks are not a homogenous group, nor do they have the unifying ideology that Marx described as necessary for group definition. In fact, black Americans are not always products of the same oppression that Cone projects for the whole race. There is, additionally, no common ideology that makes a white church white or a particular theological position white and not black. This misunderstanding of Marxian language undermines the attempted use of Marx in black theology.

Since causation is dialectical rather than mechanistic, according to Marx, outcomes are not necessarily predictive, derivative, or determinative. For example, the economics of white theologians do not exclusively determine their theological outlook; this is so

---

[99]Ibid., 68.
[100]Ibid., 71.
[101]Black liberation theology does not represent an entirely homogenous ideology regarding the use of Marxism. See J. Deotis Roberts, *Black Theology in Dialogue* (Philadelphia: Westminster Press, 1987), 41–42.

because of "the interactions among many traditions, institutions, and numerous individual strivings" involved in the theological enterprise.[102] There is too much variance among whites to determine a defined theological output.

Cone and others also misapply Marx by concluding that socioeconomic experience and monetary states determine one's perspective regarding the status of being a victim. Marx denies this idea, instead using only economic disparities to provide a *possible* explanation for why some people believe certain things. Marx would have flatly rejected the idea that economics determines perspective—the assumed characterization of white theology by black theologians. Like many readers of Marx, black theologians who promote Marx generally read his work to find perspectives advantageous to them; however, in doing so, they fail to accurately apply Marx's own doctrine (as do many "Marxists").

Marx's objection to capitalism, in many cases, is misunderstood in the black liberation theological context. Marx defines capitalism more in terms of the relationships between management and labor than in terms of the profits of a few at the expense of the oppressed others. For Marx, according to Sowell, "capital" refers to the social relations of production between persons.[103] These social relationships, to Marx, are more important than material ones. The way in which labor is extracted from the laborer is of primary concern to Marx, who stated:

> In *appearance* there is a free exchange of labor for wages, but in *essence* there is not. While a peasant performing corvee labor knows when he is working for himself and when he is working for his feudal lord, the wage worker under capitalism does not, and in fact regards the social relation in which he works as "self-evident laws of nature."[104]

There is no capitalism when workers have advantageous social and personal relations with those in management positions over them.

---

[102]Sowell, *Marxism*, 71.
[103]Ibid., 74.
[104]Marx, quoted in Sowell, *Marxism*, 75, italics his.

A novice's understanding of Marx and his view of capitalism has led black theologians to use Marxist thought to criticize capitalism in ways that Marx himself would not have done.[105] Marx understood that capitalism is a necessary part of the process of arriving at a purely socialist state. In other words, capitalism is simply one phase in the process of becoming a secure society.

Marx sees capitalism as functioning well for providing human persons with economic opportunities, but he rejects what he sees as the long-term consequences of the system—namely, that capitalism would lead some to victimize others.[106] Moreover, for Marx, socialism is possible because of capitalism. Black theologians' use of Marx to attack America's economic system is not necessarily the perspective Marx would take in attacking that very same system.

Again, capitalism provides the solid economic preconditions for socialism and communism.[107] Unlike many later Marxists, Marx himself has a great appreciation for the economic platform that capitalism provides—namely, an expanded set of options that gives people freedom to develop their potential and interests.[108] According to Sowell, Marx's concern is that capitalism is not sustainable and, in the long run, will benefit only a few "while keeping workers overworked despite labor-saving machinery."[109] The internal stresses of free enterprise lead Marx to believe that impersonality will result.

Marx also believes that any system can be used as an arm of oppression, but this belief is not recognized in the underdeveloped Marxist thought of black theologians. Sowell highlights the fact that for both Marx and Engels, any state "was an organ of coercion."[110] It seems, then, that black theologians who promote Marxism are only anticapitalistic and fail to understand that coercion is possible

---

[105]Many Marx scholars comment on the fact that Marx actually viewed capitalism as a good for a certain time. See Katz, *From Feudalism to Capitalism: Marxian Theories of Class Struggle and Social Change*, 176.

[106]See Anthony Giddens, *Capitalism and Modern Social Theory: An Analysis of the Writings of Marx, Durkheim, and Max Weber* (Cambridge: Cambridge University Press, 1971), 60–64.

[107]Sowell, *Marxism*, 76.

[108]Peffer cites Marxist scholars Robert Tucker and Allen Woods, who conclude that Marx did not condemn capitalism as unjust. See Peffer, *Marxism, Morality, and Social Justice*, 334.

[109]Sowell, *Marxism*, 78.

[110]Sowell, *Marxism*, 143.

in any form of government. Moreover, governmental control is no better than corporate control in many cases. Trading off one for the other is not necessarily better; it's simply different. It is certainly possible that one can become a victim of any political or economic structure. The critical question when examining economic equity is whether human persons are able to exercise their abilities to make choices about how best to meet their needs in accordance with human dignity.

It is government that provides the conditions that enable a given class's continued dominance. Government structures allow for various groups to oppress others. As a result, trading one type of context for another will not eliminate the possibility of new victims, nor will it erase economic distinctions between "us" and "them." Therefore Cone's and West's desire for a regime-type replacement will not necessarily produce those desired results.

The type of revolution promoted by Cone and West, suggests Sowell, would have been condemned by Marx himself. Sowell notes, "To the French workers in 1870, on the eve of the uprising that produced the Paris Commune, Marx advised against an uprising as a 'desperate folly' and urged instead: 'Let them calmly and resolutely improve the opportunities of Republican liberty.'"[111] Revolutionary change occurs through time-tested processes of refinement rather than through abrupt, violent activities.

THE LIMITS OF MARX VERSUS MARXISM FOR BLACK LIBERATION THEOLOGY

The initial attacks launched by black theologians against the "white church" produced a revolutionary spirit that Cone later found to be ineffective and regrettable. Reflecting back on the early perspectives of black theology, Cone laments the negative overreaction to white racism, which limited the black theological vision from being nothing more than a reaction to one's enemy.[112] Early black theology lacked good social analysis, including a more broad application of

---

[111]Ibid., 144.
[112]Cone, *For My People*, 87.

the doctrine of sin.[113] Additionally, there was a lack of good economic analysis, which Cone believes Marx would have provided. All of these later reflections bring to light the truth of Marx's contention that aggressive reactionaries lose credibility and are, in the end, ineffectual at persuading others to embrace their cause. One wonders if Cone and other black theologians deeply studied Marx or if they simply relied on a cursory understanding of Marxist rhetoric in developing their ideas.

Sowell reminds us that true Marxists believe that a "proletarian revolution might lead to a more democratic state, but it [will] not change the essential nature of the state as an organ of oppression."[114] More directly applied to theology, a theology dominated by "white" needs will be no less oppressive than a theology focused on the poverty and oppression of people of color.[115]

According to Sowell, true Marxists would likely tone down the revolutionary rhetoric offered by black theologians. Quick change through revolutionary means of power plays and overhauls of control is not what Marx meant by revolution; however, that has been the posture adopted by many black theologians promoting Marx's ideas. To say that Marxist revolution is needed is to say that over time, through existing processes and means, change should be directed at certain political and economic ends. This time-tested approach is what Marx sought, but it is not what black theologians promote.

Contrary to West's assessment of capitalism, Marx interprets capitalism as a force that draws the masses into the political arena and into political struggle. Marx views capitalism as an ally in securing certain freedoms for workers, not as a normative instrument for oppression.

Perhaps what is most odd about black theology's use of Marxist thought to develop a voice for the poor and the oppressed is that Marx himself did not emerge from a context of poverty

---

[113]Ibid., 88.
[114]Sowell, *Marxism*, 148.
[115]See James H. Cone, *Black Theology and Black Power* (San Francisco: Harper Collins, 1989) and Kelly Brown Douglas, *The Black Christ* (Maryknoll, NY: Orbis Books, 1994).

and oppression. Black theologians argue that only those who have been poor and oppressed themselves can speak accurately for the poor and oppressed; yet Karl Marx was born and raised in a context of affluence.[116] West criticizes Latin American theologians for speaking from a place of affluence; yet West never criticizes Marx for being a member of the class of oppressors. Sowell points out that Marx

> was born in the little German town of Trier in the Rhineland in 1818, in a three-story townhouse in a fashionable part of town. A Baron lived nearby, and his four-year-old daughter was destined to become Karl Marx's wife. The people who signed as witnesses on Karl Marx's birth certificate were prominent citizens. The Marxes, like their neighbors and friends, had servants, property, education, and local prominence.[117]

Karl Marx's father was an attorney who owned vineyards and real estate to supplement his income.[118] Marx grew up as a "spoiled" child who would regularly take walks with the learned Baron von Westphalen, discussing Homer, Shakespeare, Voltaire, and other great writers—not quite the expected lifestyle of the economic spokesman for the poor and the oppressed.[119] Marx went on to attend the then-prestigious University of Berlin, after which he pursued his doctorate at the University of Jena.

As stated earlier, Marx's connection to the controlling class should disqualify him as a figurehead for theologians of the oppressed. But, using selective rejection of certain thinkers because of their backgrounds in black theology, black theologians allow Marx to speak on behalf of those he could not relate to from personal experience. Like Marx, graduate-school-educated black professors and pastors lament about being victims in a country that has provided them with the best opportunities in the world. In most other countries in the world, it is impossible to make a living

---

[116]Francis Wheen, *Karl Marx: A Life* (New York: W. W. Norton and Company, 2000), 11–30. See also Robert Payne, *Marx* (New York: Simon & Schuster, 1968), 17–24.
[117]Sowell, *Marxism*, 164.
[118]Ibid., 165.
[119]Ibid., 166.

as a theologian. Black theologians, as Cone and others would later reflect, are just as disconnected from the oppressed as many white theologians are.[120]

The Marxian legacy is most challenging because of the unclear and sometimes contradictory differences between Marx and Marxism. Sowell's clarification of Marx, however, will help in discerning his views' actual usefulness for black theology and prevent the misuse of his ideas. For example, Marx, in his writings, pushes aside the important question of the actual source of capital. Capital is a product of labor and does not exist in a vacuum. Capital and resources are acquired, not distributed. Countries with "efficient labor and more entrepreneurship tend to have vastly higher standards of living, including shorter hours for their workers."[121] In the end, though, transferring and redistributing other people's income does not necessarily solve social and economic problems. Unsurprisingly, Sowell notes, "Large transfers of [money] to Third World countries, through nationalization and foreign aid, have often been only a prelude to the deterioration of that capital."[122] Economic growth, as demonstrated in the rise of Germany and Japan after World War II, "demonstrated that physical capital is only a product of mental capital—organization and cooperation."[123] This key understanding is found wanting in the economic reflections of black theology.

Cornel West advocates a strong relationship between black theology and Marxist thought because of their shared focus on the plight of the exploited and oppressed of the world. However, West and others need to ask a few questions: Is Marxism the only system with a focus on the poor and oppressed, or are there better alternatives that are consistent with Christian anthropology? Out of all the possible systems of thought that speak to issues of oppression, why choose Marxism? Why do black theologians overlook the options within Christianity that speak to the needs of the poor and

---

[120]Hopkins, *Heart and Head*, 159–171.
[121]Sowell, *Marxism*, 192.
[122]Ibid.
[123]Ibid.

oppressed?[124] It seems that many of these theologians considered an extremely narrow base of resources to arrive at their adopted methodologies. Perhaps if these theologians had a broader knowledge of historical theology, they would not have had to resort to Marx, nor would they have developed erroneous conclusions about white theology exclusively being for the bourgeois.[125]

West and others, in constructing a picture of what a just society would look like, move in and out of critical category distinctions. For many black scholars, true liberation comes when blacks are in control of decision-making processes at major institutions. However, this approach amounts to nothing more than defining liberation in terms of power. If blacks can lord power over others, then they are free. This narrow definition provides an endless ground for critiques of all institutions not controlled by blacks. Using a narrow, unjustified approach such as this creates a context in which it is easy to label as racist or oppressive any structure or organization in which blacks are not participating in the decision making. In a world of true racial equality, then, members of every ethnic group would need to sit on the boards of every organization and institution in order for those groups to be considered free. Such arbitrary requirements lead to ridiculous and impossible conclusions.

West rightly sees that class bifurcations in America supersede and transcend racial ones.[126] Using class to explain all of the problems in the church seeks an overly simplistic explanation that doesn't provide much information at all. With the various implications of human fallenness and institutional blindness, it is simply impossible to look solely through the lens of class (or race) to explain the state of things or to devise prescriptions for improvement.

Cone must be applauded for the courage to critique not only the early stages of his own work but also his colleagues' poorly

---

[124]See David J. O'Brien and Thomas A. Shannon, eds., *Catholic Social Thought: The Documentary Heritage* (Maryknoll, NY: Orbis Books, 1992).

[125]For example, the Baptist and Methodist traditions in the American South historically have included many poor and uneducated whites.

[126]See Jim Goad, *The Redneck Manifesto: How Hillbillies, Hicks, and White Trash Became America's Scapegoats* (New York: Touchstone, 1997). See also Lawrence Otis Graham, *Our Kind of People: Inside America's Black Upper Class* (New York: Harper Perennial, 2000).

devised solutions to social issues. Unfortunately, through his early work Cone set the trajectory, and his successors have not fully followed his later recommendations. For example, in his dealings with Marxists, Cone came to realize that Marxism, like any other system, is incapable of dealing with racism.

The *new* problem with Marxism, in Cone's view, is that it is too narrow and is unconcerned with blacks. Marxism is too dominated by whites, and unless it deals directly with blacks, it is no more than European Marxism. However, had Cone rightly understood Marxism, this racial absence would not have been a surprise. The fact is that what makes a system oppressive is not the system necessarily, but rather the actors in that system, whether those actors are evangelicals or liberation theologians. With these many internal inconsistencies and problems, the Marxism of black theology is nothing more than an ideology with Marxist rhetoric. It is not true Marxist thought at all.

FALLACIES UNDERMINING MARXIST METHODOLOGIES FOR VICTIMOLOGY

A closer examination of Marxism as a system exposes some of the methodological problems with attempting to import the system into a theological framework. Black liberation theologians adopt the class warfare motif, apply it to racial categories in the American experience, and attempt to reconcile the tensions, quite unsuccessfully. Cone, West, and others commit the means-of-production fallacy in attempting to apply a Marxist framework to social ethics in black theology. At the outset of their reflection, they assume that the means of production are controlled by white management in multinational corporations when, in fact, production is a function of the skill, ability, and intelligence of the laborers.[127] Sowell notes:

> [W]orkers' skills and experience are also major elements of a country's capital stock. The invisibility of this capital makes it difficult to determine how much of a capitalist nation's capital stock

---

[127]Thomas Sowell, *Basic Economics: A Citizen's Guide to the Economy* (New York: Basic Books, 2003), 127–147.

is in fact owned by the workers. . . . Countries whose workers lack industrial skills and experience may have massive unemployment or underemployment, and yet be unable to fill jobs created by new industries.[128]

Human capital is more than just skills, for skills can be learned. Rather, personal and cultural habits toward life and work lead some cultures and groups to excel more quickly than others.

A more basic victimologist fallacy is the belief that capital and wealth are functions of material objects rather than functions of the inherent value of the human person—i.e., human capital. What makes some nations wealthier than others is related to the dispersed skills and expertise of human persons freely engaged in creating goods. These goods become cheaper over time, as Marx predicted. According to Sowell, "Marx was one of the few socialists to understand that economic competition, motivated by 'greed,' was what drove prices down under capitalism as capitalists ceaselessly searched for more profits by seeking cheaper ways of producing than those possessed by their fellow capitalist rivals."[129] This motivation, in the end, allows more people to acquire a higher quality of goods and services. However, both Cone and West reject this function of capitalism, maintaining that wealth and human capital are separate entities.

Internationally speaking, the redistribution of international resources will not necessarily solve economic disparities, especially when those resources are redistributed into the corrupt systems of many developing nations. Black theologians' call for redistribution reveals a fallacy that many have accepted—the notion that what demarcates wealth from poverty is solely the quantity of financial capital. The International Monetary Fund and World Bank have given generous foreign aid to several corrupt regimes in the developing world, and yet poverty persists in those areas. Again, it is not the system that is corrupt and needs change; it is the actors. The focus

---

[128]Ibid., 194.
[129]Ibid., 196.

on economies of redistribution is a critical Marxist ideological flaw adopted by black theologians.

Moreover, the idea that third-party observers can define how people should think, act, feel, work, and evolve is the basis of totalitarianism and, inadvertently, is an idea promoted by readers of Marx.[130] Black theologians are guilty of narrowing, to the point of being unjustifiable, the conditions for a humane society. To so closely control human development in order to eliminate alienation may in the end produce the very alienation sought to be alleviated as people are no longer free to make decisions for themselves. Controlling the decisions of others too closely for the sake of the supposed greater good was demonstrated in the Marxist regimes of Lenin, Hitler, Castro, Ho Chi Minh, and others. None of these regimes would likely be lauded by black theologians.

CONCLUSION

A close study of Marxism exposes that black liberation theologians have adopted a form of Marxist analysis that assumes a set of presuppositions grounded in human autonomy. Like Marx, Cone writes in abstractions and broad generalizations often assumed to be facts. Cone easily uses terms such as "all" and "every" to apply to the thoughts and actions of white churches and theologians, but he provides no evidence of "all" and "every."

Cone's use of Marx and Marxist thought raises interesting problems. One of the problems centers on the inaccuracies inherent in using Marx to explain the thoughts and actions of white theologians and white churches. Additionally, the use of Marx in black theology would be objectionable to Marx himself. In fact, black theologians' treatment of Marx confirms Sowell's contention about the widespread misunderstanding of Marx's thought.

Is it true that a person's perspective is a determined product of his environment? Cone views this as a cardinal rule, and he is more than willing to apply it to white theologians. However, as stated

---

[130]Ibid., 203.

earlier, if this were true, Marx himself would be disqualified from speaking to issues of the poor and oppressed, having come from the "ruling class" himself. Moreover, history does not indicate that this claim is necessarily true.

Cone equates his understanding of "the oppressed" with the Marxist idea of alienation, resulting in a misapplication of what Marx intended. Marx believes that workers are alienated because they have no control over their employment decisions, thus leaving them humiliated. Cone, on the other hand, is not as concerned about the relationship between management and employees as he is about the relationship between races. A more accurate application of Marxist thought regarding social structures would lead to an evaluation of the relationship between church leaders and parishioners in hierarchical church bodies. Cone, then, wrongly adopts Marx's method of analysis by concluding that since blacks are alienated, Marxism is useful for addressing the problem. The critical question never fully examined by black theologians who promote the use of Marx is whether the black condition in America is analogous to the socioeconomic condition of the proletariat of whom Marx wrote. Otherwise, serious problems abound.

Problems concerning correct interpretation raise important questions. For example, is it true that white sociopolitical interests always drive the theological exposition of white theologians? One assumption by black liberation theologians promoting the use of Marx is that all whites are the same, both in their political affinities and in their economic backgrounds. Karl Marx would disagree with the assessment that all whites are of the same class by noting that in order for there to be a specific class of people, that group must have the same ideology. Even the last few years of historical theology developed in America reveal just how far from reality that is, even for whites.

An additional question is whether or not it is true that "white theology" is bourgeois theology and therefore promotes the victimizing of minorities. Are all white theologians wealthy? Is it true that "all" white theologians are by-products of a commitment to bourgeois lifestyles? Cone makes such statements repeatedly without offering any proof. Perhaps his experience almost exclusively with Ivy League theologians caused him to overlook the fact that the larger Christian community has not been, and is not, a bourgeois-only community of faith. Granted, one of the great mysteries of the Western church is slavery. Valid questions regarding Christian support and/or silence over the transatlantic slave trade, chattel slavery in the United States, the Jim Crow era, and the lack of involvement in the civil rights movement abound in black church circles. Moreover, how could a group so committed to the gospel and to righteousness (the "white" church) either support or overlook nearly 350 years of injustice?

The basis for seeking to understand this phenomena is found by seeking to discern whether or not silence on the part of many white conservative churches during slavery, reconstruction, and legalized segregation implied some sort of tacit approval. Cone concludes that those white theologians who said nothing about slavery and segregation must have implicitly supported the practice. How could it be otherwise? Because whites were given legal preference in America until 1965, Cone concludes that such a privileged position determined the theology that was produced. In other words, white theologians wrote in such a way to maintain their dominance over minorities in America and to justify that dominance theologically. A question that black theologians must wrestle with in this context is: Does silence necessarily mean tacit approval? If so, Cone's charge is fitting. If not, another more nuanced explanation must be offered.[131]

Again, Cone's charge that white theologians write only for the ruling class of white people is untenable and originates solely from a victimologist standpoint. However, suggesting that a better method for writing theology is to enlist blacks to write for the oppressed results in the same problem: using socioeconomics to drive one's theological reflection. It seems that for Cone, using socioeconomics

---

[131]Other possibilities abound but fall outside the scope of this book.

to determine the norms of black theology is legitimate (since blacks are oppressed), but white theologians' doing the same is unacceptable. It would seem that the goal of theologians' reflection on social justice should be to remove socioeconomics from the application of biblical exegesis in order to arrive at the most accurate understanding possible for the sake of Christian solidarity, regardless of economic status.

Cone and other black liberation theologians rest on the unproven idea that all white churches and theologians side with white wealth. What is most disconcerting about Cone's reflections is his lack of confidence in the Scriptures and the tradition of the church to provide sufficient tools for analyzing culture. According to Cone, Christianity, by its very nature, needs help in doing cultural analysis, and Marxism is a better and more accurate method of discerning the gap between appearance and reality than Christianity could possibly provide. For many, a dependence on Marxism significantly undermines the very premise of what the church is about. Does the church need Marx to see the world correctly?

In the final analysis, we find that the Marxism lauded by black theologians is actually not Marx's Marxism but a different system entirely, a system of their own making. Marx is used by black theologians, but their lack of understanding of some of the main points of Marxist thought damages their credibility. In the end, what is evident is that embracing the presuppositions and anthropology of victimology, grounded in the autonomy of the human experience, resulted in a social ethic separate from a Christian, biblical vision of human community.

5

Biblical Interpretation and the Black Experience

That the perception of God who allows slavery, who allows rape, who allows misogyny, who allows sodomy, who allows murder of a people, lynching, that's not the God of the people being lynched and sodomized and raped, and carried away into a foreign country. Same thing you find in Psalm 137. That those people who are carried away into slavery have a very different concept of what it means to be the people of God than the ones who carried them away.[1]

REV. JEREMIAH WRIGHT

✝

As noted in chapter 2, James Cone influenced a rejection of traditional approaches in the black church context to biblical interpretation (hermeneutics) on grounds that those interpretations derived from oppressors and were too Anglocentric. That is, they did not emerge out of an authentic black experience in America. The sources and norms of black theology come out of a perspective of the black person as victim and must reject, in Cone's view, any corruptive influence of white thought. Because of past misapplications of Scripture by conservative theologians, the black liberation theological academy is suspicious of white conservative hermeneutics. James Cone inaugurates a hermeneutic trajectory that seeks to interpret the Bible using black history, black culture, and the black experience in America. It is the purpose of this chapter to demonstrate that one can arrive at both an understanding and application

---

[1]Quoted on TV program *Bill Moyers Journal*, April 25, 2008.

of the biblical text by employing a culturally applied hermeneutic. This is possible while retaining the authority of Scripture without compromising cultural specificity.

James Cone and those who followed him jettison too many traditional orthodox Christian foundations in their desire to apply the Bible to the black experience and concomitantly often confuse interpretation methods with application methods. A culturally applied hermeneutic proceeds from a particular cultural anthropology and drives biblical exposition toward contextualization. A culturally applied hermeneutic seeks not to derive autonomous meaning from the text but rather to understand and apply meaning in particular social contexts. It is possible to understand cultural hermeneutics as a subset of biblical hermeneutics. Establishing an understanding of the African-American context as Cone and others see it provides a more cogent cognizance of issues related to comprehending and applying the Bible to the black experience. We will examine the objections by liberation theologians to "conservative," "Eurocentric" hermeneutics and will respond with critiques that maintain the infallibility and inerrancy of the biblical story. We will then seek to develop specific principles for applying an African-American, culturally applied hermeneutic that embraces many observations of the black experience among black theologians while remaining faithful to the authority of Scripture.

BLACK CHURCH HISTORY, CULTURAL ANTHROPOLOGY, AND CONTEXTUALIZATION

To begin to understand the role of the Christian church in the African-American experience, one must revisit the history of Western slavery in Africa and its practice in the United States. The African-American church began in the context of slavery as slave masters shared a portion of the gospel with slaves.[2] The Christianization of slaves was understood by some as another form of colonialism for the United States. In actuality, dehumanization of slaves resulted

---

[2]Albert J. Raboteau, *Slave Religion: The "Invisible Institution" in the Antebellum South* (Oxford: Oxford University Press, 2004), 95–150.

as slave masters denied them full understanding of their humanity in Christ. Instead the slaves were taught that their situation was a curse from God because of their blackness, an extension of the larger curse of Ham as discussed later in this chapter.[3] Slaves were consequently taught to hate themselves and their culture.

White missionaries taught the slaves not to be concerned with their present circumstances but to be concerned exclusively with eschatological issues. Even after the emancipation of the slaves, "white theology," as many describe it, failed to acknowledge the humanity of African-Americans, perpetuating a theological system of white supremacy. The nineteenth-century systematic and exegetical dehumanization of African-Americans by theologians such as R. L. Dabney demonstrates dramatically the nature of the objection to "conservative theology" by many black liberation theologians.[4]

Following the Civil War, blacks sought ways to reconcile Christianity with a culture of segregation and a Christian community split on issues of race. It was during the civil rights movement that black theologians, by developing a liberation theology, would depict Christian faith in light of the struggle for freedom.[5]

Initially, black liberation theologians were simply trying to make sense of the black experience in North America. Vinay Samuel and Chris Sugden, quoting Charles Kraft, explain that studies in cultural anthropology examine the worldview that forms a society's basic model of reality from which the conceptual and behavioral forms, linguistics, and social, religious, and technical structures find their meaning.[6] Only recently in the history of this country has African-American culture been appreciated and promoted.

---

[3]James Cone, *Black Theology and Black Power* (New York: Seabury Press, 1989), 74. See Genesis 9:20–27.

[4]R. L. Dabney, *A Defense of Virginia and the South* (Harrisburg, VA: Sprinkle Publications, 1991). Dabney, a Presbyterian racist admired by many, systematically and exegetically defends the institution of slavery, which dehumanized African-Americans. In this book, written in 1867, he refers to African-Americans as "morally inferior" and refers to the white race as a "nobler race" (281). See also Joseph Washington, *Anti-Blackness in English Puritan Religion 1500–1800* (New York: Edwin Mellon Press, 1984).

[5]Albert J. Raboteau, *Canaan Land: A Religious History of African Americans* (Oxford: Oxford University Press, 2001).

[6]Vinay Samuel and Chris Sugden, "Current Trends in Theology: A Third World Guide," Part 1, *Missionalia* 10:2 (August 1982): 64.

Understanding and appreciating an African-American cultural anthropology is germane to understanding hermeneutical issues in the African-American church.

For the African-American community, as Carl Ellis suggests, the model of reality, having been born in slavery and legal segregation, produces conceptual and behavioral forms such as Ebonics, characteristic worship styles, aphorisms, family structures, community issues, and the like that incontrovertibly possess significant intercommunity value.[7] These forms have a definite etiology, and denying the import of these forms in the larger African-American community moves toward invalidation of a necessary cultural anthropology.

Carl Ellis reminds us that the central theme in the flow of African-American history has been the quest for freedom and dignity.[8] Michael Cartwright maintains that slaves developed a different hermeneutic because "they were tired of listening to Euro-American preachers who appeared to read 'Obey your masters' over every page of the Bible. . . . [Therefore] African-Americans rejected their masters' interpretation of the Bible."[9] An African-American cultural anthropology explains how a history of slavery, segregation, racism, and dehumanization has affected the psychology of an entire people group. In the minds of liberation theologians, for the dominant culture to weigh the worth, value, and significance of another culture based on criteria that validate the dominant culture moves toward dehumanization of the less dominant culture. Many black liberation theologians argue that for Western theology to determine all hermeneutical issues and methodology for all people groups based on Anglo understandings of reality moves toward a very unfortunate reduction. William McClain protests:

> The pernicious phenomenon of fundamentalist ideology calls on African Americans to embrace a biblical authority and a reading

---

[7]Carl Ellis, Jr., *Free at Last: the Gospel in the African-American Experience* (Downers Grove, IL: InterVarsity Press, 1996), 38–50.
[8]Ibid., 30.
[9]Michael G. Cartwright, "Ideology and the Interpretation of the Bible in the African-American Christian Tradition," *Modern Theology* 9 (April 1993): 142.

and interpretation of the text without respect for the historical experiences of the African Americans in this country and people of color around the world. Relativizing race and culture as factors in religious faith and practice, this scalping ideology cuts at the very heart of the African American community, the black church, the life-giving center of black self-confidence and pride. This unsanitary surgical knife threatens to butcher the African American preaching tradition and leave it lame and limp.[10]

In Cone's era, as Ellis confirms, many early black power advocates "were justified in rejecting White Christianity-ism and asserting that we should replace White definitions of us with definitions of our own."[11] Ellis maintains that even during the civil rights movement, mainline, Bible-believing Christians misunderstood Martin Luther King, "the fundamentalists and evangelicals primarily because of their defective theological position and the Reformed Christians primarily because of their defective cultural position."[12]

In light of African-American history and cultural anthropological contextualization, then, there comes a necessary mode for communicating the truths found in Scripture to people of a different culture than that of Scripture. Contextualization is necessary, says Harvie Conn, because it is a covenant activity taking place between the "already" of redemption accomplished in Christ and the "not yet" of redemption still to be consummated. It reminds us of the ease with which our perceptions of the gospel can be deeply influenced by unconscious impositions of cultural and sociostructural perspectives on the biblical data.[13]

The truths of Scripture must be directly applied to African-American culture and put into a form that lends itself to understanding and subsequent application. By contextualizing specifically for various black communities, "theologizing becomes more than the effective communication of the content of the gospel to the cultural

---

[10]William B. McClain, "African American Preaching and the Bible: Biblical Authority or Biblical Literalism," *Journal of the Interdenominational Theological Center* 49:2 (Winter/Spring 1992–1993): 73.

[11]Ellis, *Free at Last*, 21.

[12]Ibid., 83.

[13]Harvie Conn, *Eternal Word and Changing Worlds: Theology, Anthropology, and Mission in Trialogue* (Grand Rapids, MI: Zondervan, 1984), 226.

context; it becomes the process of the covenant conscientization of the whole people of God to the hermeneutical obligations of the gospel," argues Conn.[14]

Herein lies the dilemma regarding hermeneutics: How does the African-American exegete go about the task of understanding and applying the Bible in light of an African-American cultural anthropology? What is the relationship between contextualization and hermeneutics in the African-American church? With a historical and cultural framework fully developed, the relationship between hermeneutics and African-American culture can be examined more closely, leading to the development of a culturally specific method of hermeneutics. But first we will examine why there has been such a vociferous attack on "conservative theology" and hermeneutics by black liberation theologians.

OBJECTIONS TO "EUROCENTRIC" CONSERVATIVE HERMENEUTICS

Black theologians have raised many objections to the absence of methods that interpret and apply the Bible in light of the "black experience as victim."[15] Two such objections will be examined at length in this section: slavery and Eurocentrism. These objections significantly contribute to understanding the predilection for a unique African-American hermeneutical system.[16] As intimated in chapter 3, black liberation theology locates orthopraxis in the dialectic interaction of reflection and action in the concreteness of history by reducing its motivations ultimately to the economic and social bifurcations of Marxism.[17]

---

[14]Ibid., 231.

[15]Reginald Davis, "African-American Interpretation of Scripture," *The Journal of Religious Thought* 57–58:2–2 (2005): 93–105. Also see Teresa E. Snorton, "Conjuring Liberation: African-American Resistance to Racism and Oppression," *Journal of Pastoral Theology* 14:2 (Fall 2004): 1–3. See also Alex Milulish, "Mapping 'Whiteness': The Complexity of Racial Formation and the Subversive Moral Imagination of the 'Motley Crowd,'" *Journal of the Society of Christian Ethics* 25:1 (Spring-Summer 2005): 99–122.

[16]Cain Hope Felder, "Beyond Eurocentric Biblical Interpretation: Reshaping Racial and Cultural Lenses," *Journal of the Interdenominational Theological Center* 26:1 (Fall 1998): 17–32 and "Afrocentrism, the Bible, and the Politics of Difference," *The Princeton Seminary Bulletin* 15:2 (1994): 131–142.

[17]Conn, *Eternal Word and Changing Worlds*, 232.

A question that continues to confound African-American Christians is how white Christians with clear consciences were able to use their Christianity systematically to dehumanize, oppress, and hold racist views toward African-Americans from the time of slavery through the Civil Rights Movement and beyond.[18] Moreover, why has racism not been an obvious sin in American historical theology? The empirical evidence is overwhelming that American slavery was not effaced by those who are generally considered the greatest biblical preachers and theologians of their era.[19] White male exegetes are "wittingly or not, accomplices of and contribute to the maintenance of patriarchalism, racism, apartheid, and oppression in a variety of its psychological, social, economic, or cultural forms."[20]

The whole basis of the Christian dehumanization of enslaved Africans was an illegitimate view of humanity—a view in which skin color determined not only a person's status but indeed the presence or lack of the image of God.[21] Many whites simply believed that blacks had no soul, and therefore they classified them as nonhuman. For example, many who held to the authority of Scripture used "the curse of Ham" in two ways, as Michael Cartwright demonstrates:

> First, they argued that Genesis 9:25 demonstrated that God, *not* human beings, had inaugurated the institution of human bondage, and that this arrangement was to be perpetuated through all time. Secondly, they argued that Noah's curse singled out African-Americans for perpetual service to the white race.[22]

Especially after the American Civil War, white clergymen used "the curse of Ham" to fight the notion of racial equality and the rights that would accompany such equality (voting, education, etc.).[23]

---

[18]James Cone, "Calling Oppressors to Account for Four Centuries of Terror," *Currents in Theology and Mission* 3 (June 2004): 179–186.

[19]Jonathan Edwards, Cotton Mather, and Samuel Hopkins, to name a few. See also E. Franklin Frazier, *The Negro Church in America* (New York: Schocken Books, 1974).

[20]Daniel Patte and Gary Phillips, "A Fundamental Condition for the Ethical Accountability in the Teaching of the Bible by White Male Exegetes: Recovering and Claiming the Specificity of Our Perspective," *Scriptura* 9 (1991): 8.

[21]Ellis, *Free at Last*, 43.

[22]Cartwright, "Ideology and the Interpretation of the Bible in the African-American Christian Tradition," 146, italics his.

[23]J. Daniel Hayes, *From Every People and Nation: A Biblical Theology of Race* (Downers Grove, IL: InterVarsity Press, 2003), 51–56. Even Keil and Delitzsch believed that the slavery of Africans

This misuse of Scripture by orthodox Christians prompted many during the time of slavery and beyond to seek alternative methods of biblical interpretation. Black Christians began to develop an indigenous theological outlook and practice.[24] For example, in light of this previous misuse, Ron Liburd rejects the authority of Scripture:

> If for no other reason, the patent flawed anthropology in the Bible—which the powerful have exploited in order to oppress women, blacks, and other people in the plantation, industrial, and technological economy—is justification for rejecting the confounded notion of the Bible as the Word of God.[25]

It is this use of Scripture in American historical theology that abrogates the use of conservative hermeneutical principles—e.g., that the Bible has authority as divinely inspired and that the Bible is the rule of faith and reason—in the black theological academy.

My intention, far from defending the past misuse of Scripture by those who hold to a traditional hermeneutical methodology, is to object to the rejection of traditional hermeneutics on that basis alone.[26] The objection may be summarized this way: Because those who held to the inerrancy, infallibility, and authority of the Bible also used the Bible as a theological basis for maintaining slavery, oppression, racial segregation, and dehumanization, any conservative hermeneutical method associated with that tradition perpetuates Eurocentric hegemony and must, therefore, be rejected as a valid system for use in an African-American ecclesiastical construct.[27]

---

was a fulfillment of this curse. They write, "In the sin of Ham there lies the great stain of the whole Hamitic race, whose chief characteristic is sexual sin; and the curse which Noah pronounced upon this sin still rests upon the race . . . the remainder of the Hamitic tribes either shared the same fate, or sigh still, like the Negroes, for example, and other African tribes, beneath the yoke of the most crushing slavery." C. F. Keil and F. Delitzsch, *Commentary on the Old Testament* (Grand Rapids, MI: Eerdmans, 1986), 157–158.

[24]Ellis, *Free at Last*, 47.

[25]Ron Liburd, "Like . . . a House upon the Sand: African American Biblical Hermeneutics in Perspective," *Journal of the Interdenominational Theological Center* 22:1 (Fall 1994): 89.

[26]R. L. Dabney writes, "Since it is not self-evident, not a necessary, not a universally received truth, that slavery is sinful, we therefore claim the authority of the Scriptures as conclusive," in *A Defense of Virginia and the South*, 211–212. Statements like this raise questions about the datum that Scripture is the rule of faith and reason.

[27]See Cain H. Felder, "Biblical Hermeneutics and the Black Church Tradition," *Union Seminary Quarterly* 42:1–2 (1988): 63; William H. Myers, "The Hermeneutical Dilemma of the African American Biblical Student," in *Stony the Road We Trod: African American Biblical Interpretation*, ed. Cain H. Felder (Minneapolis: Fortress Press, 1991), 44–50; Robert A Bennett, "Biblical Hermeneutics

Because a particular methodology has been used to dehumanize and oppress people of non-European descent for several hundred years, any associations with that particular hermeneutical tradition, then, is rendered impotent in an African-American, African, or Latino setting. This objection is raised *ad nauseum.* This objection, however, is valid in the sense that it raises questions about the cultural biases used in the application, a biblical doctrine of man in Protestant historical theology. How, for example, is it possible to maintain a biblically derived doctrine of man—viz., the *imago Dei*—and concurrently dehumanize other human beings? History demonstrates that this can be done in good conscience, however, if those who are being dehumanized are not considered human. The inferiority of the African was a *de facto* assumption, especially in the theological traditions of Protestants in the West.[28]

Although a tendentiously appropriated misapplication of Scripture to maintain Anglo cultural ascendancy warrants such a reaction, the rejection of conservative hermeneutics on that basis alone presents a *non sequitur.* This objection establishes itself on a hasty generalization. To this objection one might reply, *abusus usum non tollit* (abuse does not negate proper use). "Conservative" hermeneutics was not necessarily the problem, although one could build a *prima facie* case based on misapplications. The objection, rather, should fall on *individual* abusers or traditions rather than on the hermeneutical principles as a whole. The principles themselves were not responsible for odious misuses of Scripture.

Suppose an African-American was run over by a white racist driving a red car. What, then, would be the object of any disapprobation? Would it be the white racist or the red car? The object of any discommendation would be the white racist, not the red car. Using *a posteriori* logic to conclude that the future use of traditional herme-

---

and the Black Preacher," *Journal of the Interdenominational Theological Center* 1:2 (Spring 1974): 39; and Osayande Obery Hendricks, "Guerrilla Exegesis: A Post-Modern Proposal for Insurgent African-American Biblical Interpretation," *Journal of the Interdenominational Theological Center* 22:1 (Fall 1994): 92. The most dramatic rejection has been proffered by Ron Liburd, "Like . . . a House upon the Sand: African American Biblical Hermeneutics in Perspective," 71–91.

[28]James Cone, "The White Church and Black Power," in *Black Theology: A Documentary History, Volume I, 1966–1979,* ed. James H. Cone and Gayraud S. Wilmore (Maryknoll, NY: Orbis Books, 1979), 120–121. See also Dabney, *A Defense of Virginia and the South,* 288.

neutical principles will lead to oppression and subsequently to rejection of traditional hermeneutical principles based on previous misuse ultimately fails. Using this logic, however, one could conclude that not only is the white racist to be condemned, but all red cars should be rejected as well. Both red cars and white racists must universally be repudiated. In the same way, then, the claim that conservative hermeneutical principles—viz., the authority of Scripture, its inerrancy, and its infallibility—are to be rejected based on past misuse is inherently problematic. In the next section we will see how hermeneutical principles associated with "conservative" theologians are in fact most appropriate, holistically, in an African-American context.

Another objection initiated by Cone and other black liberation theologians is that traditional hermeneutics and theology are Eurocentric, and therefore their Anglo-cultural norms are inapplicable to any African-American context. Cain Hope Felder believes there is much "biblical study that goes on in North America and other regions besides Europe, but the conventions, the standards, the procedures, and the assumptions of biblical scholarship, like those of nearly every field, have been set and fixed by white, male, European academics over the past several centuries."[29] As such, the task of biblical interpretation must flow from a desire to resist "Euro-American domination."[30] Since white, male, Eurocentric scholarship is flawed by imperialism and is irrelevant to black churches, "black scholars must challenge the Eurocentric mind-set not only for the sake of the black community but also for the health of *all* scholarship."[31]

American evangelical theologians, generally speaking, tend to be concerned about applications of Scripture in an Anglocultural context. Because whites are the dominant cultural group, black liberation theologians and others argue that whites assume theological and/or social issues are germane to every cultural representation in America. This type of hegemony only interacts, then, with

---

[29]Felder, ed., *Stony the Road We Trod: African American Biblical Interpretation*, 6.
[30]Ibid.
[31]Ibid., 6–7, italics his.

polemical issues in Anglo culture. Moises Silva writes in response to the liberalism of biblical interpretation that "one can no longer assume that an individual who professes an evangelical faith will hold the 'party line' on key social and ethical issues such as capital punishment, abortion, nuclear armament, divorce, premarital sex, or homosexuality."[32] These issues may not be seen universally as the highest priority of all Christians of various races.[33] While obviously important, are these to be "key" ethical issues for every cultural grouping in America? Furthermore, in order to be considered an evangelical Christian, must one's sociological interests rest in those areas in particular? The charge of ecclesiastical hegemony and theological colonialism rests on this type of assumption by Angloconservative theologians—viz., "our" issues are universally important to any theological school of thought.

The charge against Anglo theologians is that they determine what the polemical issues are for everyone without acknowledging the possibility of a different perspective on what those polemical issues would, in fact, include.[34] This may be construed as cultural arrogance, as only those things that affect Anglo models of reality dominate the discussion. What Anglo theologians fail to do is dialogue with other cultures. There exists a general understanding of what is meant by "our" culture that presumes upon the definition of "our." The range of meaning of "our culture" used by Anglo theologians is not necessarily meant to include issues pertinent to African-American, Latino, or Asian constructs. This is evidenced by which issues are proffered as important. Currently the concern is that traditional conservative theology does not deal with issues germane to the African-American context such as slavery, racism, unemployment, the status of African-American men, drug abuse, welfare, affirmative action, etc.[35]

---

[32]Moises Silva, "Has the Church Misread the Bible?" in *Foundations of Contemporary Interpretation*, ed. Moises Silva (Grand Rapids, MI: Zondervan, 1996), 18.
[33]Ibid. See also David Kuo, *Tempting Faith: An Inside Story of Political Seduction* (New York: Free Press, 2006), 266.
[34]Ellis, *Free at Last*, 81–84.
[35]Anthony Carter, *On Being Black and Reformed: A New Perspective on the African-American Christian Experience* (Phillipsburg, NJ: P&R, 2003), 69–118.

As intimated previously, some black theologians understand the Eurocentric variation as perpetually misapplying the *imago Dei*. Gosnell Yorke writes, "In some Christian theological circles, it is now a truism that God may have made us in God's own image (Gen 1:26) but that in our theologizing about who God is, we inevitably end up, to varying degrees, making God in our image as well—be it consciously or subconsciously."[36] Because the image of God is offered, in many instances, as European in origin, the important issues of the entire kingdom are those of high priority in Anglo culture. Simply stated, Eurocentric values and norms are not necessarily adaptable to all cultural contexts.[37] Takatso Mofokeng comments:

> The denominational theologies which were developed elsewhere in response to social and religious challenges of other social settings are found to be inadequate and incapable of explaining the harsh realities of deepening repression of black Christians by white Christians.[38]

The rejection of traditional hermeneutical principles rests on the assumption that those principles are not useful in an African-American context. To this, we may raise the description versus explanation objection.[39] The notion that Eurocentric principles are inapplicable is meant to serve as sufficient explanatory evidence for rejection of all things white. However, several questions must be raised that are not articulated in the black liberation theologians' objections. Among them, what are the distinctions of a Eurocentric theology of methodology that are only applicable to Anglocultural constructs? How specifically is the authority of Scripture an impediment to African-American Christians? What makes a datum Eurocentric? How exactly does biblical orthodoxy

---

[36]Gosnell L.O.R. Yorke, "Biblical Hermeneutics: An Afrocentric Perspective," *The Journal of Religious Thought* 52:1 (Summer/Fall 1995): 3.

[37]Brain Blount, *Cultural Interpretation: Reorienting New Testament Criticism* (Minneapolis: Fortress Press, 1995), 3.

[38]Takatso Mofokeng, "Hermeneutical Explorations for Black Christology," in *Exploring Afro-Christology*, ed. John Samuel Pobee (New York: Peter Lang, 1992), 85.

[39]Owen Flanagan, *The Science of the Mind*, 2nd ed. (Cambridge: The MIT Press, 1991), 129.

perpetuate ecclesiastical colonialism? In many instances, expressing objections against Eurocentric theology simply knocks down straw men. What African-American critics have failed to do is explain how Eurocentric theology is applicable to Anglo contexts and not applicable to their own. How is the systematizing of the providence of God, for example, applicable to Anglo-American culture and not applicable to an African-American context?

Scholars concede that there is more than one way of approaching the task of understanding and applying biblical texts in light of differentiated social contexts. By understanding that the truth can be approached by multiple routes, we come to appreciate the contribution of different perspectives outside of our own. Vern Poythress offers cogent, fresh perspectives on this issue:

> People who think in terms of covenant theology may not think that there are really alternatives. In a sense, if covenant theology is right, there are no other alternatives. That is, no system contradicting covenant theology can possibly be right. But a contradictory system is not the only alternative—there could also be complementary ways of expounding the same truths. If we chose to do it another way, there would be differences of emphasis and differences in organization, but not contradiction. . . . Hence I conclude that since we do not always observe everything and see all the angles, it is perhaps better not to put all our eggs in one basket.
>
> That is to say, it is better not to use only one analogy or theme as the route by which we approach biblical interpretation. If we do, we may miss something. . . . [We] must be ready to listen to other people in the body of Christ whom God has gifted in other ways. Men have to listen to women and women to men; scholars to non-scholars and vice-versa; Americans to Latinos and vice-versa. We therefore must listen to other people with other perspectives.[40]

---

[40]Vern Poythress, "Science and Hermeneutics," in *Foundations of Contemporary Interpretation*, ed. Moises Silva, 514–516. Other scholars, in the larger scope of theological study, have identified the challenge to avoid hegemony in their exegetical work. See Bernard Lategan, "The Challenge of Contextuality," *Scriptura* 9 (1991): 4 and Daniel Patte and Gary Phillips, "A Fundamental Condition for Ethical Accountability in the Teaching of the Bible by White Male Exegetes: Recovering and Claiming the Specificity of Our Perspective," *Scriptura* 9 (1991): 7–28. V. Phillips Long makes a distinction between truth claim and truth value that I found helpful (see "The Art of Biblical History," in *Foundations of Contemporary Interpretation*, 297–298).

This is quite profound because Poythress acknowledges and promotes the contribution of other perspectives—not only different theological perspectives but also cultural ones. While the challenge of predetermining the meaning of the text is usually put only in theological terms, Poythress's challenge expands to cultural relevancy and encourages intercultural dialogue. Poythress's comment also helps establish the philosophy behind the necessity of cultural hermeneutics.

A culturally applied hermeneutic, whether it be African-American, Latino, or Asian, only describes various audiences and subcultures to whom the truth of the self-attesting Scriptures is to be applied. With particular target audiences, texts may be applied differently. However, it may be a different "angle" or emphasis and not necessarily contradictory to the "party line" interpretation. A culturally applied hermeneutic, which brings a particular cultural anthropology into consideration, may be the most effective means to achieve the task of contextualization. By engaging the contributions from other perspectives, understanding and applying the Scriptures in God's multiethnic, international kingdom would be much more of a realization than an ideological discussion.[41] Instead black liberation theologians chose to develop a separate ideological, theological, and hermeneutical framework.[42]

THE ALTERNATIVE: LIBERATION AND WOMANIST HERMENEUTICS

As we have seen, black liberation theologians bring certain elements of the text into prominence, like a black consciousness construed as victim, and those texts concerning the liberation of the oppressed in general.[43] Cone and others reference the Exodus as the meta-

---

[41]See William H. Myers, "The Hermeneutical Dilemma of the African American Biblical Student," in *Stony the Road We Trod: African American Biblical Interpretation*, ed. Felder, 40–47. For more on issues related to multiracial contributions to theological education, see J. Deotis Roberts, "And We Are Not Saved: A Black Theologian Looks at Theological Education," *Religious Education* 87:3 (Summer 1992): 353–369.

[42]See Will Coleman, *Tribal Talk: Black Theology, Hermeneutics, and African/American Ways of "Telling the Story"* (University Park, PA: Pennsylvania State University Press, 1999).

[43]Silva, "Has the Church Misread the Bible?" 119. See also Diana L. Hayes, "James Cone's Hermeneutic of Language and Black Theology," *Theological Studies* 61:4 (December 2000): 609–631.

narrative for the black experience in America. For black liberation theologians, James Cone lays out the first principles for understanding the Word of God in relation to God himself. First, the Christian understanding of God arises from the biblical view of revelation, a revelation of God that takes place in the liberation of oppressed Israel and is completed in the Incarnation, in Jesus Christ. Second, God in black theology must be the God who is participating in the liberation of the oppressed of the land because God has been revealed in the history of oppressed Israel and decisively in the Oppressed One, Jesus Christ. It is impossible to say anything about God without seeing him as being involved in the contemporary liberation of all oppressed peoples, which puts Cone's ideas about hermeneutics into perspective.[44]

Cone later develops the idea that the social context of African-Americans drives interpretation because "unlike white theologians, who spoke to and for the culture of the ruling class, black people's religious ideas were shaped by the cultural and political existence of the victims in North America."[45] Cone sets the platform for future theologians plagued by victimology to view the task of hermeneutics this way:

> [T]he hermeneutical principle for an exegesis of the Scriptures is the revelation of God in Christ as the Liberator of the oppressed from social oppression and political struggle, wherein the poor recognize that their fight against poverty and injustice is not only consistent with the gospel but is the gospel of Jesus Christ.[46]

Hermeneutics, then, is carved out of the presupposition of the human person as a victim of social and political oppression above all else. Cone has established the orientation for black liberation hermeneutics for years to come. "The Black Hermeneutical School," inaugurated by black theologians such as Charles B. Copher and James Cone, crafted a method of interpretation to ensure consistency with

---

[44]James Cone, *A Black Theology of Liberation* (Maryknoll, NY: Orbis Books, 1990), 60–61.
[45]James Cone, *God of the Oppressed* (San Francisco: Harper San Francisco, 1975), 53.
[46]Ibid., 81–82.

the theme of liberation for oppressed African-Americans.[47] As noted in chapter 2, liberation is the hermeneutical content of black theology. Biblical texts are used to bear witness to God's liberating activity so that stories in the black experience in America are also authoritative (such as slave testimonies, black folklore, personal narratives, and so on).[48]

When the experience of blacks in America is broadened to issues beyond race, Cone asserts that black liberation theology positions itself to "come out of the closet and take a stand with human beings who are struggling for liberation," fighting for the liberation of women, homosexuals, "mother earth," and lower economic classes' struggle against the upper classes.[49] Any black person who is a victim of social or political oppression of any kind is a candidate for rightly inculcating the methods of black liberation theology.

God's self-disclosure, for black liberation theologians, is found in African-American history as the lens through which African-Americans have come to know and understand God in the centuries-old struggle against oppression.[50] In a watermark text on black hermeneutics, Cain Hope Felder laments that the black church has tended to imitate popular evangelical white churches, thus distorting and misappropriating the biblical text to ignore issues central to the black experience.[51] Connecting the black experience in America with the story of the Exodus and the exilic experience of Israel provides the hermeneutical orientation for interpreting the black experience of being a victim.

While Cone introduced the connection with the Israelites'

---

[47]Frederick Ware, *Methodologies of Black Theology* (Cleveland: Pilgrim Press, 2002), 28. Also see Charles Copher, *Black Biblical Studies: An Anthology of Charles B. Copher* (Chicago: Black Light Fellowship, 1993), 66–77 and Gosnell L.O.R. Yorke, "Biblical Hermeneutics: An Afrocentric Perspective," 1–13.

[48]Ware, *Methodologies of Black Theology*, 35. Also see Larry L. Enis, "Blackening the Bible: The Aims of African American Biblical Scholarship," *Interpretation* 60:1 (January 2006): 110–112.

[49]James H. Cone and Gayraud Wilmore, eds., *Black Theology: A Documentary History, Volume II: 1980–1992* (Maryknoll, NY: Orbis Books, 1993), 2–3.

[50]Ware, *Methodologies of Black Theology*, 41. The oppression primarily referenced is oppression of blacks around the world by whites of European descent.

[51]Cain Hope Felder, *Troubling Biblical Waters: Race, Class, and Family* (Maryknoll, NY: Orbis Books, 1989), 79.

Exodus experience, later black theologians embraced the Exile. Joseph Crockett maintains that the theme of exile as a focusing lens for teaching Scripture from a black perspective "allows us as African-American Christians to be faithful to our history and experience."[52] The Exile serves as a reference in making sense, it is believed, of the dispersion of Africans during the era of the international slave trade. Crockett continues, "The exile provides a perspective so that persons may embrace a history that includes being stolen, sold into captivity, and transported to and transplanted in an alien land."[53] Black theologians fundamentally believe that white theologians are simply incapable of employing just methods of biblical interpretation for the black community because "[white people] continue to speak from the vantage point of the majority culture or dominant culture, and they impose the dominant world view on the existential realities of other cultures."[54]

Therefore, a primary responsibility of the African-American exegete is to aid the African-American believing community in understanding, surviving, and altering its present sociopolitical situation through accurate and appropriate interpretation and application.[55] The "black experience as victim" exercises hermeneutical control over the Bible so the black church can articulate an appropriate self-understanding as black, maintain its integrity as a separate community, and determine its mission in the world. This is because no other institution or organization can possibly claim to be able to articulate African-Americans' collective yearnings and aspirations.[56]

What black hermeneutics seeks to do is validate, in part, the connection between Africa and African-Americans. Africans and people of African descent must be understood as having made significant

---

[52]Joseph Crockett, *Teaching Scripture from an African-American Perspective* (Nashville: Disciple Resources, 1991), 16.

[53]Ibid.

[54]Ibid., 57.

[55]William H. Myers, "The Hermeneutical Dilemma of the African American Biblical Student," in *Stony the Road We Trod: African American Biblical Interpretation*, 44. See also Osayande Obery Hendricks, "Guerrilla Exegesis: A Post-Modern Proposal for Insurgent African-American Interpretation," *Journal of the Interdenominational Theological Center* 22:1 (Fall 1994): 93.

[56]Vincent Wimbush, "Historical/Cultural Criticism as Liberation: A Proposal for an African American Biblical Hermeneutic," *Semeia* 47 (1989): 48.

contributions to world civilization, as well as to the biblical story, as proactive subjects within history.[57] African-American biblical interpretation, Felder argues, redirects the focus of the biblical story away from Europe toward the continent of Africa in three ways: (1) It reconsiders the maps of ancient Bible lands with respect to their proximity to Africa instead of Europe. "In the Bible," says Felder, "there is not a single mentioning of either England or Germany; by contrast, however, countries in Africa (Egypt, Cush, Put, Punt, etc.) are mentioned again and again."[58] (2) Human civilization began in Africa. "The Garden of Eden story . . . indicates that the first two rivers of Eden are closely associated with ancient Cush, the Hebrew term that the Greeks would later transpose as 'Aithiops' or Ethiopia (meaning literally 'burnt face people')."[59] The rivers mentioned in Genesis 2, which surround the whole land of Cush/Ethiopia, place the story within the continent of Africa, not Europe. (3) "The ancient land of Canaan was an extension of the African land mass and in biblical times African peoples frequently migrated from the continent proper through Canaan/Palestine toward the east (including Asia), namely the 'fertile crescent' or Tigris and Euphrates rivers of Mesopotamia," which again orients the biblical story toward Africa, not Europe.[60]

Likewise, the salvation history of the biblical story includes many Africans that white scholarship has not acknowledged. Eurocentric theologians tend to deny, overlook, or minimize the fact that black people are in any significant way part of the Bible itself.[61] A distinct black hermeneutic approach seeks to rectify this oversight.[62]

---

[57]Felder, "Cultural Ideology, Afrocentrism, and Biblical Interpretation," in Cone and Wilmore, eds., *Black Theology: A Documentary History, Volume II: 1980–1992*, 188. See also Robert A. Bennett, "Biblical Hermeneutics and the Black Preacher," *Journal of the Interdenominational Theological Center* 1:2 (Spring 1974): 38–53.

[58]Ibid., 189.

[59]Ibid.

[60]Ibid.

[61]Ibid.

[62]See Walter A. McCray, *The Black Presence in the Bible: Discovering the Black and African Identity of Biblical Persons and Nations* (Chicago: Bible Light Fellowship, 1995) and John L. Johnson, *500 Questions and Answers on the Black Presence in the Bible* (St. Louis: Johnson Books, 2002).

WOMANIST INTERPRETATION

Another post-Conian development in hermeneutics within black liberation theology is the womanist hermeneutical school.[63] Womanist theology is both an affirmation and critique of black male theologians. Like their black male colleagues, they issue a critique of white supremacy. Womanists are generally black female theologians within the black liberation theology milieu who tend to distance themselves from white feminist theologians, criticizing them for ignoring racism. For this reason, womanist theologians find themselves more at home with black men who endeavor to struggle against white supremacy in the church, the academy, and society. Even so, the felicity between womanist and black male theologians should not be reduced to a monolithic solidarity. Jacquelyn Grant, considered by many as the founder of womanist theology, reminds us of the special place of black women, saying, "It would not be very difficult to argue that since Black women are the poorest of the poor, the most oppressed of the oppressed, their experience provides a most fruitful context for doing Black Theology."[64]

Although they laud the accomplishments of their male colleagues, womanist theologians criticize black male theologians for ignoring the devastating effects of patriarchy—a system of oppression that, from the womanist perspective, has been "as destructive to the freedom of the human community as racism."[65] In this way, womanist theologians join hands, though not without reticence, with white feminist theologians. Here we will briefly survey the role that Conian victimology played in the development of womanist theology by examining the works of three stalwarts among womanist theologians: Delores Williams, Katie Cannon, and Cheryl Sanders.[66] James Cone originally launched the presupposition of

---

[63]For the most recent and scathing critique of womanist hermeneutics, see Alistair Kee, *The Rise and Demise of Black Theology* (Aldershot, UK: Ashgate Publishing, 2006), 100–127, 168–189.
[64]"Black Theology and Black Women," in *Black Theology: A Documentary History, Volume I, 1966–1979*, ed. James H. Cone and Gayraud S. Wilmore (Maryknoll, NY: Orbis Books, 1979), 428.
[65]James H. Cone, "Womanist Theology: Introduction," in *Black Theology: A Documentary History, Vol. II*, 257.
[66]See Delores S. Williams, *Sisters in the Wilderness*, 2nd ed. (Maryknoll, NY: Orbis Books, 1995); Delores S. Williams, "Searching for a Balm in Gilead," *Living Pulpit* 9:4 (October-December

the authoritative self-sufficiency of black female consciousness construed as "victim" that supplies the theological anthropology for womanist theology.

Thus far it would seem that the *modus operandi* for defining womanist theology is railed in along a *via negativa*—i.e., *Womanist theology is not x*. Some might argue that this conclusion is not completely unmerited and is further corroborated by the words of James Cone:

> The Blackness of their experience means that White women do not know what Black women know even though their gender is the same. . . . Womanists' identity as women means that Black men do not know what Black women know even though their race is the same.[67]

Even so, Cone insists that womanist theology is not dependent upon negative definitions. Womanist theology is more than a conjunction of black male liberationist and white feminist conclusions. Rather, womanist theology is centrally defined by the black women's right to "name [her] own experience and to develop a way of doing theology accountable to the survival and liberation of black women."[68] That experience, says Cone, is not exhausted by reference to gender or racial oppression.

In order to illumine the experience of black women, womanists look to resources that "touch the essence of their identity as human beings."[69] Womanist theologians continue in the Conian framework, grounding theology in the self-sufficiency of black consciousness construed as victim. The most notable and ubiquitous of these resources have been the writings, reflections, and lived experiences

---

2000): 6; Delores S. Williams, "A Theology of Advocacy for Women," *Church & Society* 91:2 (November-December 2000): 8; Katie G. Cannon, *Black Womanist Ethics* (Eugene, OR: Wipf & Stock, 1998), 4; Katie G. Cannon, "Womanist Perspectival Discourse and Cannon Formation," *Journal of Feminist Studies in Religion* 9 (Spring-Fall 1993): 30; Cheryl Sanders, "Ethics and the Educational Achievements of Black Women," *Religion and Intellectual Life* 5 (Summer 1988): 8; Cheryl Sanders, *Empowerment Ethics for a Liberated People: A Path to African American Social Transformation* (Minneapolis: Fortress Press, 1995), 7; Cheryl Sanders, "Afrocentrism and Womanism in the Seminary," *Christianity and Crisis* 52 (April 1992): 124; and Ware, *Methodologies of Black Theology*, 24, 155–156.

[67] Cone, "Womanist Theology," 257.
[68] Ibid.
[69] Ibid., 263.

of Alice Walker and Zora Neale Hurston. The writings of Alice Walker have been particularly formative for self-identified womanist theologians. Her book *In Search of Our Mother's Gardens: Womanist Prose* (1983) is the aegis of the term *womanist*. The frequency with which Walker's definition of the term continues to be debated among black women scholars is proof of her lasting influence in the womanist tradition. What follows is an examination of how key womanist theologians, adopting a victimologist perspective, sought to advance the application of black liberation theology to black women.

Ware rightly notes that black womanist hermeneutics within black liberation theology argues for the primacy of the African-American woman's experience, spirituality, biography, and literature in theological discourse. African-American women's experience provides the correct hermeneutical starting point, separate from the patriarchal history of black theologians and the racism of white feminist theologians.[70] Delores Williams provides an excellent example. Williams's anthropological presuppositions directly and significantly shape her biblical hermeneutic and her understanding of culture. At the heart of Williams's anthropology is the insistence that black women ought to love themselves exclusively. Concretely this means that black women ought to have the right to name their own experience—to interpret the human person and consequently all of reality however they so choose.

In formulating her definition of the human person, Williams adopts victimology as the core of human identity. Therefore, Williams's biblical and cultural interpretation proceeds upon the basic assumption that priority must be given to whichever interpretations mitigate the oppression of black women. In Williams's own words, the appropriateness of womanist theological conclusions

> will ultimately reside in [their] ability to bring black women's history, culture, and religious experience into the interpretive circle of Christian theology and into the liturgical life of the church.

---

[70]Ware, *Methodologies of Black Theology*, 40.

> Womanist theological language must, in this sense, be an instrument for social and theological change in church and society.[71]

Williams would agree with other black theologians who believe that to know God is to know about ourselves and that this is what revelation means to black people. Even so, Williams suspects black male theologians of androcentrism and therefore insists that "black liberation theology's understanding . . . of revelation . . . holds very little promise for black women. A complete revisionist approach in [this area] of black liberation is needed if black women are ever to be included."[72] Therefore, Williams would indubitably alter Cone's maxim to say: *For black women, to know God is to know about themselves as victims. This is what revelation means to black women.* If revelation consists in an investigation and prioritization of "the black female condition," then only those portions of the Bible that "identify and reflect upon those biblical stories in which poor oppressed women had a special encounter with divine emissaries of God"[73] are regarded as significant.

Overall, the black liberation hermeneutic approach considers normative and primary: (1) the black experience and its role in sacred history; (2) the belief that God is a God of liberation and is therefore black; and (3) the central message of the biblical text as liberation and the necessity of interpreting and applying it as such. The black experience is the final authority in the interpretation and application of the biblical texts, and both are judged against how well they contribute to the liberation of oppressed African-Americans in general and men and women respectively.[74]

An important question, and one arguably difficult to quantify, is, does the hermeneutic developed by the black liberation tradition accomplish the type of interpretation it desires? We may confidently answer no. The pitfall of orienting a theological system in this way

---

[71] Delores S. Williams, "Womanist Theology: Black Women's Voices," *Christianity and Crisis* (March 2,1987), 270.
[72] Williams, *Sisters in the Wilderness*, 169.
[73] Williams, "Womanist Theology: Black Women's Voices," 271.
[74] Ware, *Methodologies of Black Theology*, 64. See James H. Evans Jr., *We Have Been Believers: An African-American Systematic Theology* (Minneapolis: Fortress Press, 1992), 11–52 and Blount, *Can I Get a Witness: Reading Revelation through African American Culture*, 41–67.

is that it predisposes a system of arriving at conclusions that often redefine Christianity autonomously to a form that many would find biblically unrecognizable.

Kevin Vanhoozer, in response to liberation hermeneutics in general, reminds us of the postmodern affinities in the rejection and critique of orthodox hermeneutical approaches. In the opinion of black liberation theologians, the real perpetrators of interpretive violence are those "who maintain that there is a right (and thus a wrong) way to read. What is deemed oppressive in the context of postmodern hermeneutics is the claim that there is such a thing as a morality of interpretation and universal norms, rather than a plurality of ethical claims."[75] The irony, of course, is the objection to a Eurocentric mode of interpretation while replacing it with an Afrocentric one. A narrow, culturally driven hermeneutic is only permissible if it is an African-American one, it is claimed. Many questions ensue: does the black liberation denial of culturally transcendent hermeneutical principles lead to more freedom or less? Does the reader's liberation from white oppressive traditions and Eurocentric determinative texts lead to a genuine freedom or to a new form of slavery (and to an older form of interpretive oppression initially objected to, namely, eisegesis)?[76] How are Afrocentric absolutist interpretations different from a white, Eurocentric "oppressive" one in terms of accurately understanding and applying the biblical text to an African-American context and beyond?

Simply stated, if the biblical text has no integrity of its own outside of the black experience, then readers are free to do whatever they want with it, which takes us back to our starting point, the misuse of Scripture by the "oppressors." Readers are then free to ignore what the text actually says and to reinterpret it so they have whatever convenient meaning they want to hear.[77] We see this in the progression from nineteenth-century theological liberalism to

---

[75]Kevin Vanhoozer, *Is There Meaning in the Text?: The Bible, the Reader, and the Morality of Literary Knowledge* (Grand Rapids, MI: Zondervan, 1998), 162–163.
[76]Ibid.
[77]Ibid., 164.

black liberation theology to womanist theology to black gay/lesbian liberation theology.[78]

Such interpretive authority, grounded in experience, comes at the expense of the biblical text itself. The biblical text only has meaning insofar as it submits to the autonomy of the black experience, making the interpreters like gods defining meaning rather than creatures receiving meaning.[79] In the end, the biblical text is held hostage to a victimization of its own: loosely playing to the interpretive interests of special interest groups. How can the text and the biblical story be protected from the oppressive tendency to interpret the Scriptures through the experiences of some while prohibiting the voices of others? Does claiming the black experience as authoritative make it so? Is there a third way?

The remainder of this chapter attempts to introduce principles for rethinking black hermeneutics, maintaining orthodox principles of hermeneutics while understanding and applying the biblical story in light of past abuses by "white" theologians and abuses by a form of Afrocentrism (i.e., the black experience in America). Proper uses of contextualization and application can provide a platform for applying the biblical story to the unique particularities of the black experience without jettisoning orthodox understandings of the absolute authority of Scripture and the inerrant, inspired, self-attesting, condescended revelation of the triune God to his people.

PRINCIPLES FOR PROPER CONTEXTUALIZATION FOR A CULTURALLY APPLIED HERMENEUTIC

Contextualization is a dynamic process of the church's reflection, with the Incarnation and God's condescension in communicating to his people as ultimate paradigms, applied in obedience to Christ and his mission in the world. This includes interaction with the

---

[78]Stanley J. Grenz and Roger E. Olson, *20th Century Theology: God and the World in a Transitional Age* (Downers Grove, IL: InterVarsity Press, 1992), 200–236 and Dwight N. Hopkins, *Heart and Head: Black Theology—Past, Present, and Future* (New York: Palgrave, 2002), 173–193.

[79]Davis, "African-American Interpretation of Scripture," 104.

text of Scripture as the Word of God and the context as a specific human situation.[80] The interpreters may be part of the context or, as cross-cultural communicators, represent a second context in a three-way process.[81]

As Silva points out, contextualization reminds us of the relativity of our interpretation, "because we are weak, limited, ignorant, and sinful. God's truth remains sure, while our perception of that truth may need to change."[82] Contextualization has been abused in discussions of hermeneutics, but the basic concept remains necessary because of the distance between the world of the Bible and our own. Silva maintains that the question "is not whether we should contextualize, for we all do it, but rather how to do it without compromising the integrity of the Bible."[83] Contextualization implies not that the interpreter creates meaning but that the interpretation of the biblical story involves its application to respective contemporary situations, including racial groups.[84]

Richard Muller offers critical principles for appropriating a contextualized approach that does not result in relativism. Muller is correct to highlight the fact that in order for the gospel to become meaningful to us in our present life situation and to others in different places and different cultures, it must be brought into diverse contexts of the modern world.[85] Contextualization is not new to Christians. It has from the beginning been a necessary component of the spread of Christianity, since the missionary work to the Greek-speaking world of the ancient Mediterranean basin and then to the Latin world of the western Mediterranean.[86] However, much black liberation theology has erred in its misdirected attempt at contextualization and has confused application with interpretation.

---

[80]"Contextualization," in Sinclair Ferguson, ed., *Dictionary of Theology* (Downers Grove, IL: InterVarsity Press, 1988), 164.
[81]Ibid.
[82]Silva, "Has the Church Misread the Bible?," 30. See also Harvie M. Conn, "The Missionary Task of Theology: A Love/Hate Relationship?" *Westminster Theological Journal* 45:1 (1983): 1–21 and *Eternal Word and Changing Worlds: Theology, Anthropology, and Mission in Trialogue.*
[83]Silva, "Has the Church Misread the Bible?" 76.
[84]Tremper Longman III, "Literary Approaches to Biblical Interpretation," in *Foundations of Contemporary Interpretation*, 120.
[85]Richard Muller, "The Study of Theology," in *Foundations of Contemporary Interpretation*, 654.
[86]Ibid.

For a cultural hermeneutic applied to various African-American contexts, Muller reminds us that cultural anthropology remains important but is not the final authority. The significance of a document or concept, argues Muller, arises out of the relationship already existing between the interpreter's self-understanding and the framework of understanding lodged in the document or concept.[87] What black liberation theologians objected to is the fact that their white colleagues never provided a platform for applying the Scriptures within the confines of an African-American's self-understanding. This occurred because Christians tend to view their own confessional or theological systems as absolute, whereas what is needed are systematic presentations of theology that "ought to strive for diversity of expression (as if diversity in and of itself were a virtue)."[88] The point is not that particular cultures have better systematic presentations than others, but that "within a given culture or society, one systematic presentation will best express the biblical message at the heart of Christianity."[89]

Contextualization allows us to avoid absolutizing a particular formulaic presentation of theology in such a way that it becomes identified with the biblical message as such, so that transmission of the message from one context to another or from one era to another becomes difficult or impossible. Muller argues:

> [T]he work of contextualization is little more than the self-conscious exercise of a form of historical method for the sake of the present-day statement of the faith. The result of an effective contextualization of the Christian message is no more and no less than the adaptation of the substances of Christian teaching to a new linguistic and cultural life situation. The result of a successful exercise in historical criticism is no more and no less than the understanding of the meaning of Christian teaching in a past linguistic and cultural life situation. It should be clear that the present-day effort of contextualizing a historical faith rests on an ability to grasp the meaning of the faith in its basic forms by means of historical method. Contextualization, therefore, when it

---

[87]Ibid.
[88]Ibid., 655.
[89]Ibid.

becomes a conscious exercise, is part of a historically controlled exercise in hermeneutics.[90]

When theology crosses a cultural boundary, whether histori-cal, geographical, or racial, new terms and new metaphors must be drawn out of the spiritual, intellectual, and linguistic storehouse of the culture and adapted for use in Christian theology.[91] Muller maintains that with proper contextualization, the original mean-ing does not change, but the text, the document, the doctrine, the idea or principle in question attains a significance in a new context. Therefore, to a certain extent the new context attains a new signifi-cance related to the old and at the same time broadens the horizon of the believing community across cultures in the present. The new significance is not entirely new, as if never before articulated or known, but draws on the original meaning in its original context and also on its tradition of meaning without dismissing the past, in order to expand the realm of interpretation into various cultural situations. Muller believes that the presuppositional approach is best equipped to handle cross-cultural application of the biblical story.[92]

Kevin Vanhoozer reminds us that theology is never written in a cultural vacuum but always in a particular cultural situa-tion. Contextualization is necessary. Vanhoozer, in an attempt to help those seeking to apply the truth to a specific culture avoid the human-centered autonomy of black liberation hermeneutics, provides a cogent perspective on what contextualization is not.[93] First, contextual theology is not a form of cultural relativism. It would be a misappropriation of the biblical text to exaggerate the distance between cultures past and present. Additionally, elevating one present-day culture over others, either past or present, inches toward cultural idolatry and opens the door for relativism.

Second, contextual theology is not a form of cultural determin-

---

[90]Ibid.
[91]Ibid., 658.
[92]Ibid., 660.
[93]Kevin Vanhoozer, *The Drama of Doctrine: A Canonical-Linguistic Approach to Christian Theology* (Louisville: Westminster John Knox Press, 2005), 310–314.

ism. No sociopolitical context itself takes on the role of determining truth. Cultural determinism falls prey to a form of reductionism that makes theology a mere function of surface phenomena of cultural, social, and political structures. Missing this point reduces theology to function as our sociopolitical context and encourages a victimologist perspective like that inaugurated by Cone.

Third, contextual theology is not a form of cultural absolutism. Cultural absolutism can take two forms: one is the biblicist who sees the content of Scripture as so universal that it effectively applies to all times and places as a timeless culture where contemporary culture is of little or no theological significance (nor are the diverse cultures of the biblical authors). Second is the correlationist who privileges the needs, beliefs, and values of the present cultural contexts over those of the biblical text. In this view, the concerns and questions of present cultures and subcultures set the theological agenda, which forces the biblical text to conform to the ideology of a subcultural interest group.

Lastly, contextual theology is not a form of cultural colonialism. The temptation among some is to confuse the development of theology with one's culturally conditioned understanding and application of theology. A truly contextualized theology must do more than impose one culture's categories or issues upon another, as Poythress points out.[94]

Contextualization is missiological activity even with the various subcultures in the church in America. Vanhoozer maintains that the goal of theology is to enable Christians in any and every time or culture to participate fittingly in God's triune mission to the world. In this sense, we recognize the prose of Scripture to be transcultural in significance and universal in interest to the mission of the triune God. The Bible addresses all cultures and provides the overarching theo-drama, the message of what God is doing in Christ for the sake of people in every culture in the world. For this reason, the biblical story is considered transcultural.[95]

---

[94]Poythress, "Science and Hermeneutics," 525–526.
[95]Ibid., 314.

Both Ellis and Vanhoozer speak of the precepts, principles, and paradigms that need to be maintained when engaging in contextualization.[96] *Precepts* refer to clear commands in Scripture, such as those found in the Ten Commandments. *Principles* vary because some believe that those who "principlize" often wrongly assume that what gets contextualized is a pristine, culture-free principle, when what one actually gets is one's culturally conditioned understanding of a biblical principle. Vanhoozer insists that theology is a human activity and as such does not exist in a culture-free zone. *Paradigms* are the incidents, stories, or characters that model something exemplary for Christian faith and practice. These biblical paradigms are the exemplars of faithful witness to Jesus Christ. Their testimony is true, contextually relevant, and culturally intelligible. Vanhoozer concludes by saying, "What is exemplary and *worthy* of contextualization, in other words, is the communicative praxis of Scripture itself."[97]

If Poythress, Conn, Silva, Ellis, Muller, and Vanhoozer, among others, are to be taken seriously, exploring the tension between the discipline of theology and the African-American needs to be investigated properly to ward off tendencies toward idolatry and autonomy. When culturally applied hermeneutic approaches are understood as applicatory in nature, they do not necessarily contradict the larger task of hermeneutics as it relates to the science of biblical exegesis. Culturally applied hermeneutics, which is nothing more than contextualization, complements the larger goal of hermeneutics by seeking to understand and apply the Bible in light of particular cultural anthropologies.

TOWARD AN AFRICAN-AMERICAN HERMENEUTIC: A CULTURALLY APPLIED HERMENEUTIC IN PROCESS

The black religious community has been burdened with issues that include social, political, and economic questions: wealth and poverty, power and powerlessness, privilege and oppression, whites and nonwhites.[98] Black liberation theologians have under-

---

[96] Carl Ellis, *Going Global: The Role of the Black Church in the Great Commission of Jesus Christ* (Chicago: Urban Ministries, 2005), 8. See also Vanhoozer, *The Drama of Doctrine*, 315–317.
[97] Vanhoozer, *The Drama of Doctrine*, 317.
[98] Conn, *Eternal Word*, 253.

lined the importance of these questions, argues Conn, because "white, Western evangelicals generally have not responded quickly or positively to this set of questions. Our pietist tradition segregates 'spirituality' from 'the world.' And our fear of the 'social gospel' spectre haunts our ability to formulate theology for the marginalized."[99] Silva maintains that while extreme forms of liberation theology are to be rejected, "caution must be taken regarding all forms of ideological reading on the grounds that distortion is possible or even likely; much may nevertheless be learned from these perspectives."[100] Black liberation theology brings out themes of Scripture commonly passed over by many readers of the Bible, such as concern for the poor, racial injustice, and so on.[101] Therefore, an approach is needed that is faithful to the text and faithful to applying the text to issues facing many black church communities today.

Issues of contextualization and an African-American cultural anthropology are at the forefront of the matter. As Harvie Conn argues, cultural and anthropological perspectives color and flavor theological development and categories. Our hermeneutic for understanding, says Conn, is shaped by our sociological presuppositions concerning knowledge. Conn continues:

> Personal, class, and social agendas tend to reshape the world we see and the way we see it. Aspects of reality that are uncongenial to those social interests are filtered out in the interest of self-serving alternative interpretations. Thus when theologizing is done by Western experts who by their very training (if not background) have become part of the "professional" middle- or upper-class white society, can one really expect that Western theology will see the poor and sinned-against? Theology, if it is to become truly and comprehensively communal, must emerge from a praxis of commitment to God's peace for the poor (1 Corinthians 1:27–28).[102]

If Conn is correct about the shaping of theology by sociological

---

[99]Ibid., 253–254.
[100]Silva, "Has the Church Misread the Bible?," 120.
[101]Ibid.
[102]Conn, *Eternal Word*, 254–255.

presuppositions, a culturally specific African-American hermeneutic is much in need of development.

Simply stated, African-American hermeneutical methodology can at best be described as amorphous and may seem to be protean in nature because of the diversity of perspectives on these issues within the black church.[103] James Cone helped popularize the idea for the black church:

> *The hermeneutical principle for an exegesis of the Scriptures is the revelation of God in Christ as the Liberator of the oppressed from social oppression and to political struggle, wherein the poor recognize that their fight against poverty and injustice is not only consistent with the gospel but is the gospel of Jesus Christ.*[104]

This principle, as a starting point, violates the principle of helpful contextualization described by Vanhoozer because black theology becomes relativistic, culturally determined, and culturally absolutist, creating a new form of cultural colonialism. A culture's experience is not authoritative enough to warrant its function as primary over the biblical text, nor is it objective enough to relegate Scripture subordinate to it.

In black liberation theology, the final reference point for theological development is the black experience—and that experience is the experience of racial oppression.

Considering the very diversity that exists across socioeconomic lines, one would be compelled to ask how an interpretive system predicated on a cultural ideology is simultaneously broad in scope but also narrow enough to be truly efficacious. Related questions are not easily answered. To use an interpretive system that approaches biblical interpretation within a liberation motif may not be useful to the African-American community as over time significant numbers

---

[103]Attempts at establishing a method of African-American interpretation are inconclusive. See Thomas Hoyt Jr., "Biblical Interpreters and Black Theology," in *Black Theology: A Documentary History, Volume II*, 196–209. The use of Scripture in black theology is most commonly associated with black liberation theology. See E. K. Mosothoane, "The Use of Scripture in Black Theology," in *Scripture and the Use of Scripture*, ed. W. S. Vorster (Pretoria, South Africa: University of South Africa, 1979), 28–37. See also Randall C. Bailey, *Yet with a Steady Beat: Contemporary U.S. Afrocentric Biblical Interpretation* (Boston: Brill, 2003).

[104]Cone, *God of the Oppressed*, 81–82, italics in original.

of African-Americans acquire wealth and political power. What is required is the establishment of philosophical, methodological principles of a culturally applied hermeneutic that are broad enough to apply to the African-American community at large.

Carl Ellis maintains that a culturally applied contextualized hermeneutic is necessary because "white theology" does not address the issues African-Americans face today.[105] A culturally applied black hermeneutic, suggests Bruce Fields, is needed to remind the dominant white church community that the issues of concern to the black church are commensurate with the views of members of the black theology community.[106]

How exactly might a culturally applied hermeneutic function in the larger discipline of biblical hermeneutics for the black community? Simply stated, *hermeneutics* is understood as the study of principles and methods of interpretation and *hermeneutic* as a specific perspective that may guide one's interpretive matrix.[107]

A culturally applied hermeneutic, then, can offer a specific perspective that may guide one's understanding and application—viz., in terms of a particular cultural anthropology. Cultural hermeneutics is a subset of hermeneutics. As stated earlier, this approach is purposed to be descriptive according to the adjective preceding the word *hermeneutics* (e.g., African-American, Asian, Latino, etc.). It simply describes in what context the truth is to be understood and applied. This does not limit the understanding or application to a particular cultural construct but simply identifies the recipient of the biblical exposition for clarification and for explaining any appearance of tendentious phraseology.

A culturally applied hermeneutic is not where hermeneutics begins but rather follows the work of exegesis and biblical theology.[108] After the truth principles of a text have been illumined, the interpretation

---

[105]Ellis, *Going Global*, 43.
[106]Bruce Fields, *Introducing Black Theology: Three Crucial Questions for the Evangelical Church* (Grand Rapids, MI: Baker Academic, 2001), 47–51. Bruce L. Fields, PhD, is associate professor of biblical and systematic theology at Trinity Evangelical Divinity School in Deerfield, Illinois.
[107]Walter C. Kaiser and Moises Silva, *An Introduction to Biblical Hermeneutics: The Search for Meaning* (Grand Rapids, MI: Zondervan, 1994), 285. Also see Kevin Vanhoozer, ed., *Dictionary for Theological Interpretation of the Bible* (Grand Rapids, MI: Baker Academic, 2005), 283.
[108]Kaiser and Silva, *An Introduction to Biblical Hermeneutics*, 285.

can be connected to a particularized understanding and application. This allows for the preservation of the authority of Scripture and the subordination and relevancy of cultural experience. A culturally applied hermeneutic is not meant to illumine truth principles from the text but rather to transmit biblical truth cross-culturally. In this sense, all hermeneutics is cultural hermeneutics in that biblical meaning is transferred from an ancient culture to a modern one. A culturally applied hermeneutic naturally leads to contextualization and may, in fact, simplify that process. A culturally applied hermeneutic complements the larger discipline of hermeneutics by providing a mechanism for transcultural transmission of biblical truth. With this approach the *principia theologiae* are not compromised but are specifically applied.

The emphasis on understanding and application is aided by the work of Hans-George Gadamer.[109] He argues that a culturally applied hermeneutic should be constructed in terms of seeking understanding of the text as well as remaining subordinate to the text, instead of depending on a tenuous, culturally specific interpretive methodology.[110] Gadamer explains:

> Understanding is not to be thought of so much as an action of one's subjectivity, but as the placing of oneself within a process of tradition, in which past and present are constantly fused. This is what must be expressed in hermeneutical theory, which is far too dominated by the idea of a process, a method. . . . [Hermeneutics] is not to develop a procedure of understanding, but to clarify the conditions on which understanding takes place.[111]

Although Gadamer would be considered an existentialist, his concern for not focusing hermeneutics solely on methodology helps us in our formulation of the subordinate role of a culturally applied hermeneutic to that of, say, exegesis. A culturally applied

---

[109]Poythress, "Science and Hermeneutics," 529. See Daniel Doriani, *Putting the Truth to Work: The Theory and Practice of Biblical Application* (Phillipsburg, NJ: P&R, 2001), 27. See also Vanhoozer, *The Drama of Doctrine*, 327–330. See also Vanhoozer, *Is There Meaning In This Text?*, 106–109.

[110]See Vanhoozer, *The Drama of Doctrine*, 328–329. Vanhoozer has a rightly critical assessment of Gadamer in his "Discourse of Matter: Hermeneutics and the 'Miracle' of Understanding," *International Journal of Systematic Theology* 7 (2005): 5–37.

[111]Hans-George Gadamer, *Truth and Method*, eds. Garret Barden and John Cumming, trans. Glen Doepel (New York: The Seabury Press, 1975), 258.

hermeneutic's primary concern is not necessarily method, although its use will have methodological implications, but rather contextualization.

Gadamer, also concerned with application, noted that a text, if it is to be understood properly, must be understood at every moment, in every particular situation, in a new and different way.[112] There exists a close relationship between understanding and application such that the two are not mutually exclusive. For our purposes, Gadamer's contribution helps to identify other critical issues in the study of hermeneutics. One of the ways in which his system errs is that it elevates experience as the *summum bonum* and the *sine qua non* of biblical hermeneutics instead of the self-attesting Word of the triune God. With experience as Gadamer's ultimate interpreter, his perspective has some limitations.

Gadamer's aim is to describe the conditions that make understanding possible, a question that transcends methodological considerations.[113] A culturally applied hermeneutic may be said to describe the conditions that raise appropriate questions regarding cultural analysis and application of a text. The questions raised are to be informed by seeking to bridge the gap between the culture of the Bible and current cultures.[114] Richard Muller expresses his concern this way:

> One way to approach this hermeneutical or interpretive task is to ask the question of how and why a text—any text, whether biblical, church historical, or contemporary—comes to us with an identifiable meaning that is grounded on its original historical, cultural, religious, and social milieu, how and why that meaning can be known by us, how and why that meaning, as preserved through a long history or mediated by contemporary events, yields up a significance for us in our own situation.[115]

---

[112]Ibid., 275.
[113]Theodore Kisiel, "The Happening of Tradition: The Hermeneutics of Gadamer and Heidegger," in *Hermeneutics and Praxis*, ed. Robert Hoolinger (Notre Dame, IN: The University of Notre Dame Press, 1986), 5.
[114]Daniel M. Doriani, *Getting the Message: A Plan for Interpreting and Applying the Bible* (Phillipsburg, NJ: P&R, 1996), 143–144.
[115]Richard Muller, "The Study of Theology," in *Foundations of Contemporary Interpretation*, 645.

In order to know the right questions to ask of the text in light of a particular culture, the exegete must *know* the culture to which he seeks to communicate for effective understanding and application.

In an African-American context, serious engagement with an African-American cultural anthropology is essential. One must be familiar with several issues, including the reality of American slavery, the multigenerational psychological effects of legal and ecclesiastical dehumanization, contemporary manifestations of racism, joblessness, the influence of black nationalism on African-American consciousness, the Nation of Islam, the historical dynamics of the African-American family, the modes and forms of social cohesion and stratifications in the black community, violence, illegitimacy rates, mortality rates, the role and function of the historical African-American church, black theology, womanist theology, African theology, etc.[116] For an African-American cultural hermeneutic, these issues and more will aid not in deriving truth in the exegetical task but rather in the communication of truth principles in a form that African-Americans will understand and be able to apply to their lives.[117]

The truth principles illumined from Scripture will always be transcultural, as is the Word of God itself. However, the application of biblical truth will also involve cultural specificity, whether it be Anglo, African-American, Latino, Asian, African, West Indian, etc. Certain aspects of holiness are independent of cultural specificity, but certain aspects of the pursuit of holiness can be specifically applied to particular cultures. This specificity does not necessarily contradict the larger task of hermeneutics, and many of the applications will overlap. A culturally applied hermeneutic simply enhances the communicative dimension of biblical exposition.

I have sought to outline somewhat of an ideological understanding of the role and function of a culturally applied hermeneutic and some issues related to the necessity for a particular African-American model. Four hermeneutical principles serve as a reference for using an African-American cultural hermeneutic. This is

---

[116]Ellis, *Going Global*, 79–86.
[117]Fields, *Introducing Black Theology*, 86–104.

not a methodological listing but simply a possible scheme for use in any type of culture. These principles take into account African-American history and cultural anthropology as well as issues in the African-American theological academy but can be used as the basis for constructing any cultural hermeneutic.[118]

(1) *For a culturally applied hermeneutic, Scripture must be handled as the authoritative Word of God and the rule of faith and life.*[119] Lawrence Murphy comments, "The principles and assumptions that inform black interpretation of Scripture seem to be, first, that the Bible is the authoritative Word of God and contains the eternal truths necessary for salvation."[120] Joseph Crockett understands the centrality of Scripture in the African-American church community as the primary text of the Christian community.[121] Crockett acknowledges that the primary purpose of relating the Bible's redemptive story with that of the African-American's story is to teach Scripture.[122] He explains further:

> Scripture as a frame of reference is authoritative. It serves as the referent to which all concerns are related and by which all issues are judged. For the church, scripture is the plumb of life. The church understands itself, its reason for being, and its destiny in terms of scripture. The church is the people of the Word.[123]

Until recently, the primacy of the Word of God has been a central element in the African-American church. It was the slaves' understanding of Scripture that led them to realize they were being treated in a way that was inconsistent with God's redemptive plan, regardless of

---

[118]See Peter J. Paris, "Basic African American Values: Gifts to the World," *Soundings* 81:3–4 (Fall/Winter 1998): 553–570.

[119]Warren H. Stewart offers hermeneutical principles; however, his function is in the context of liberation theology. See *Interpreting God's Word in Black Preaching* (Valley Forge, PA: Judson Press, 1984).

[120]Lawrence Murphy, "African American Worship and the Interpretation of Scripture," *Ex Auditu* 8 (1992): 97. Furthermore, even James Cone comments that "the black experience requires that Scripture be a source of Black Theology," although he would challenge the claim to the authority of Scripture over experience; *God of the Oppressed*, 31. See also Bernard Ramm, *Protestant Biblical Interpretation*, 3rd ed. (Grand Rapids, MI: Baker Books, 1970), 93–162 as he establishes the centrality of Scripture in hermeneutics and exegesis.

[121]Joseph Crockett, *Teaching Scripture from an African-American Perspective* (Nashville: Discipleship Resources, 1990), xi.

[122]Ibid., 9.

[123]Ibid.

the way the Word was being misused by Anglo Christians.[124] While some perceive the notion of biblical authority as an "impediment to black Christians,"[125] this must be rejected because it creates a false Christianity based on existentialism instead of God's revelation.

In Ellis's view, for African-Americans, a culturally applied hermeneutic begins when we "cultivate our knowledge of God and his Word, and practice obedience to God and his Word in every area of our lives."[126] God intends for African-Americans to worship God in their culture where African-American theology is a legitimate expression of the biblical message, having its historical and cultural application in the black experience, yet is firmly rooted in the universal truth of the Word of God.[127]

(2) The exegesis of the text seeks to illumine truth principles that are transcultural and precede the use of a culturally applied hermeneutic. Texts have meanings that are independent of contemporary cultural constructs, although cultural context will determine how those texts are understood and applied to particular social locations. The Bible is self-authenticating and self-attesting. The derivation of textual meaning comes from the text itself, not from meaning culturally infused into the biblical text. Scripture is self-interpreting in this sense (*scripturam ex scriptura explicandam esse*). Truth principles are not culturally dependent but rather are biblically derived from the text. Vanhoozer explains, "Christian mission and theology alike involved ministering the gospel to culture in words and acts of truth, love, and justice that correspond to, participate in, and render the prior triune mission."[128] The Scriptures are transcultural because the Bible addresses every culture with the message of the kingdom. The truth of the work and person of Christ and the kingdom of God is universal because it is able to descend into a myriad of cultures.[129]

---

[124]Cain Hope Felder, "Cultural Ideology, Afrocentrism and Biblical Interpretation," in *Black Theology: A Documentary History, Volume II: 1980–1992*, 187. See also J. Deotis Roberts, *Black Theology in Dialogue* (Philadelphia: Westminster Press, 1987), 17.

[125]Liburd, "Like a House," 79.

[126]Ellis, *Going Global*, 6.

[127]Ibid., 8–9. Ellis continues, "Through biblical precepts, principles, and practices, God's Word provides an adequate and authentic framework in which to view ourselves and understand [African-American] cultural history," 9.

[128]Vanhoozer, *The Drama of Doctrine*, 314.

[129]Ibid., 323.

(3) *The truth principles are understood and applied in light of a cultural anthropology.* The truth principles are applied in such a way that history, modes of socialization, polemical issues, etc., are used as means to communicate those principles in the most effective way. Ellis explains, "The African American community today is in desperate need of a fresh approach to theology—a theology that is true to Scripture and, at the same time, speaks to [African Americans'] current situation."[130] In an African-American frame of reference, the principles are to be applied to personal ethics as well as to social ethics.[131] Black theology's moral directives and imperatives "[have] been and always will be authoritative in the African American community and outside the community only in proportion to its faithfulness to Scripture as mediated in and through the black church."[132] The principles are to be understood and applied to issues specifically in the African-American community and across the African-American socioeconomic spectrum—i.e., from poor to wealthy. As stated previously, these issues will range from racism to the plight of the African-American male to stratifications within African-American social classes. The truth is applied with cultural specificity.

(4) *The truth principles are to be contextualized in the vernacular.* Conn maintains that "theology must be culture-specific in recognition of the receptor-oriented character of divine revelation."[133] This last principle employs the use of any necessary social or cultural conventions, specific to parts of black culture, in order to communicate most effectively for the purpose of understanding and real application.[134] The principles are to be communicated in the language of the people one seeks to reach.

---

[130]Ellis, *Going Global*, 50.

[131]The African-American clergyman has been deliberate in seeking to understand the implications of redemption from a personal perspective but also from the perspective of social structural reform in American domestic policy. See Felder, "Biblical Hermeneutics," 65; Crockett, *Teaching Scripture*, 15–26, 39–50; Roberts, "And We Are Not Saved"; Vincent Wimbush, "Historical/Cultural Criticism as Liberation: A Proposal for an African American Biblical Hermeneutic," *Semeia* 47 (1989): 52.

[132]Fields, *Introducing Black Theology*, 78.

[133]Conn, *Eternal Word*, 210. See also Cheryl A. Kirk-Duggan, "Ebonics as an Ethically Sound Discourse: A Solution, Not a Problem," *Annual of the Society of Christian Ethics* 18 (1998): 139–160.

[134]Tim Keller, "Missional Church," delivered at a Mission to North America Conference for the Presbyterian Church in America, June 2001.

CONCLUSION

Black liberation theology, with its ideological hermeneutic of victim-ology, is simply incapable of producing its desired results because it presupposes the black experience as authoritative over Scripture. While black liberation theologians offer many poignant critiques of "conservative" theology, in the end what is needed is better application of the biblical texts instead of jettisoning the absolute authority of the text because of prior misuse. America's increasing cultural diversity calls for new vistas in the field of hermeneutics. What is proposed here, using an African-American model, is the need for cultural hermeneutics in the study of interpretation. Contextualization and cultural anthropology seem to be natural considerations in the area of missions but not so within an American paradigm. Perhaps there has been a tacit assumption that because Americans occupy the same geography, understanding and applica-tion of Scripture will be the same for all people groups within that geography. The development of a separate black theology proves that this is not the case.

A culturally applied hermeneutic provides a powerful comple-ment to the study of interpretation. It allows Scripture to serve as the ultimate ground for truth while recognizing the relevance of cul-tures in understanding and applying that truth. While the African-American academy has legitimate objections against the historical use of Scripture, those objections cannot become the basis for an African-American cultural hermeneutic. We must move beyond the objections in an effort to help God's people become a mature church. Cultural relevancy remains subordinate to exegesis. The work of the kingdom of God requires that multiple cultures submit themselves to divine revelation. Cultural hermeneutics is meant to serve as a tool to understand God's calling upon the lives of his people in every community and culture.

6

Is There a Future for
Black Liberation Theology?

*Maybe now we can begin to take steps to move the black
religious tradition from the status of invisible to the status
of invaluable, not just for some black people in this country, but for all the people in this country.*

*Maybe this dialogue on race, an honest dialogue that
does not engage in denial or superficial platitudes, maybe
this dialogue on race can move the people of faith in this
country from various stages of alienation and marginalization to the exciting possibility of reconciliation.*[1]

REV. JEREMIAH WRIGHT

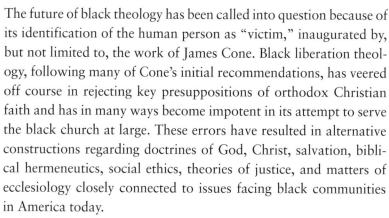

The future of black theology has been called into question because of
its identification of the human person as "victim," inaugurated by,
but not limited to, the work of James Cone. Black liberation theology, following many of Cone's initial recommendations, has veered
off course in rejecting key presuppositions of orthodox Christian
faith and has in many ways become impotent in its attempt to serve
the black church at large. These errors have resulted in alternative
constructions regarding doctrines of God, Christ, salvation, biblical hermeneutics, social ethics, theories of justice, and matters of
ecclesiology closely connected to issues facing black communities
in America today.

Black theology, in its current trajectory, has been rendered
somewhat useless to many black communities because of anti-

[1]"Reverend Wright at the National Press Club," *New York Times* (April 28, 2008); http://www.
nytimes.com/2008/04/28/us/politics/28text-wright.html?_r=2&pagewanted=2.

quated categories and its inability to adjust to the changing socio-economic patterns of black Americans—i.e., the rise of the black middle class. This chapter introduces selected recent critiques in order to demonstrate that if black theology is to have a future and any positive impact on black communities and the black church, it must be re-created in line with the key presuppositions of orthodox Christianity.

EARLY CRITIQUES BY J. DEOTIS ROBERTS

Before looking at current critiques, the future of black theology cannot be addressed without first examining the issues raised by J. Deotis Roberts, a contemporary of James Cone in the black theology movement and also a significant early critic. Roberts questioned the perspectives of both Albert Cleage and James Cone, especially Cone's method and sources. Roberts's views are vital to this discussion because many later critiques suggest points of contention already outlined in Roberts's earlier works in the 1970s. One can only wonder, if Cone had taken the advice of his colleague, would black liberation theology have avoided becoming as useless as it has become to black communities today?

For example, Roberts believed that Cone did not present or construct a theology that deals adequately with the issue of racial reconciliation.[2] Even early on in Cone's writings, "the narrowness that Cone has sought to impose upon Black Theology must be rejected."[3] Black theology is not a religion of black power and demands that "a Christian theologian is not an interpreter of the religion of Black Power. . . . But he or she is attempting to understand the Christian faith in the light of his or her people's experience."[4] Because of the universal need for reconciliation and ecumenism, Roberts did not believe that only the oppressed have the credibility to write theology. In addition, Roberts held that Cone was too influenced by the Black Power movement. For Roberts, when black the-

---

[2]Frederick L. Ware, *Methodologies of Black Theology* (Cleveland: The Pilgrim Press, 2002), 70.
[3]J. Deotis Roberts, *Liberation and Reconciliation*, 2nd ed. (Louisville: Westminster John Knox Press, 2005), 4.
[4]Ibid., 5.

ology takes reconciliation seriously, the church will have to work at the task of "intercommunication between blacks and whites under the assumption that for those who are open to truth, there may be communication from the inside out, but at the same time there may be communication from the outside in."[5] Unlike Cone, Roberts desired to see both black and white Christians work together for liberation and reconciliation on an interracial basis.

Roberts also highlighted how Cone proposed an eschatology without a "heaven" in ways associated with Islam.[6] He objected to Cone's lack of eschatology because it fails to open up the Scriptures and relate the whole gospel to the black experience.[7] Contrary to Cone, Roberts believed that what is precious in the Christian faith is "the assurance of a conscious and personal destiny. . . . Eternal life means that we are agents of liberation and reconciliation in the world and among men because we share in the love, justice, and power of God."[8]

Roberts also suggested that Cone's Barthian presuppositions would limit Cone's usefulness to black communities and the black church in America because a narrow Christocentric view of revelation that distinguishes between religion and the Christian faith is unreasonable. Roberts asserted:

> James Cone will need to break with Barthianism if he is to enter into meaningful dialogue with African theologians who are taking seriously their precolonial traditions. . . . What would be helpful is an understanding of the revelation of God as manifest in all creation and all history as measured by the supreme revelation of God.[9]

J. Deotis Roberts presented a more traditional approach, understanding the black experience that had positioned him in contradistinction to Cone and other black liberation theologians on a myriad of issues. For Roberts, Cone's "oppression-liberation" formula

---

[5]Ibid., 7.
[6]Ibid., 86.
[7]Ibid., 90.
[8]J. Deotis Roberts, *A Black Political Theology* (Philadelphia: Westminster Press, 1974), 188–189.
[9]Ibid., 20.

did not unlock the full power of the biblical story for the black church.[10] "Cone is inadequate for the contextualization of black and African theologies," argued Roberts.[11]

Roberts agreed with Cone regarding the disapprobation initiated in colonialism and racism—either or both—that gave rise to black theology. This is indisputable. His departure from Cone rests in understanding the following:

> Sin as moral evil, as it manifests itself in the brokenness in human relations (between blacks and whites), is personal and social. Blacks as well as whites must reckon with the personal and social directions of sin. . . . In the area of race it is difficult for most whites to overcome this deep-seated drive toward the worship of self. A realistic humanism requires blacks to be aware that their own togetherness is shot through with the possibility of exploitation of one another. . . . Sin as self-centeredness is a disease that inflicts the black community as well as the white community.[12]

When black liberation theology begins with the principles, patterns, and practices set forth in the redemptive history revealed in Scripture, any theological reflection will always include both social injustice and personal sin. Conian formulations rely heavily on social injustice at the expense of undermining the fact of the Fall and the fact of personal sin.

Cone discounts preaching to issues of personal, individual sin because it was that very type of preaching that distracted slaves from understanding a biblical view of social justice and pushed them toward an otherworldly mind-set in their theological understanding. Cone's reaction, however, went too far in that now many black liberation theologians do not call African-Americans to repentance for their personal sin and transgression against God. Roberts reminds us that sin is not limited merely to social injustice but bears a personal aspect as well, with respect to the righteousness of God. The gospel deals both with sin and being sinned against.

---

[10]J. Deotis Roberts, *Black Theology in Dialogue* (Philadelphia: Westminster Press, 1987), 25.
[11]Ibid., 41.
[12]Roberts, *Liberation and Reconciliation*, 57–58.

For post-Conian theologians, there is no place for personal sin in terms of personal holiness. Theology becomes an instrument of alleviating social justice without also calling people to repentance before a holy God. Jesus Christ's mission is reduced to a program of saving people from social oppression. If that were his only mission, then humanity still awaits another Messiah, the Davidic heir, to deal with personal sin as prophesied in the Scripture's prophetic literature. The Robertsian formulation at least introduced the issue of personal sin.[13] Social injustice, biblically understood, originates from personal patterns of injustice manifest at a corporate level. Corrupt and evil social structures cannot be maintained without corrupt and evil individuals managing those structures.

Much liberation theology leaves the reader with the impression that African-Americans are not accountable for personal sin and do not need a savior for their own sin, redemption, and restoration. Roberts's important contribution is simply saying that African-Americans do sin, which is central to understanding injustice. Perhaps this explains why there is little relationship between the black theological academy and the local black church.

JAMES CONE'S CRITIQUES AFTER THIRTY YEARS

In 1999, a major work, *Black Faith and Public Talk*,[14] was published to honor and critique the contribution of James Cone to black liberation theology. As Alistair Kee points out, what holds true is that black liberation theologians seem incapable of actually offering critiques of Cone's work beyond his early formulations or offering new applications in light of the new socioeconomic realities of black communities.[15] The 1999 edition of this book was a disappointing and missed opportunity for black liberation theology to address

---

[13]For further discussion regarding the contrast in Conian and Robertsian theological methodology, see James H. Evans Jr., *We Have Been Believers* (Minneapolis: Fortress Press, 1992), 110–112; Diana L Hayes, *And Still We Rise: An Introduction to Black Liberation Theology* (New York: Paulist Press, 1996), 109–113; James Cone, *God of the Oppressed* (San Francisco: Harper Collins, 1975), 239–240; and Roberts, *Black Theology in Dialogue*, 41–47.
[14]*Black Faith and Public Talk: Critical Essays on James H. Cone's Black Theology and Black Power*, ed. Dwight N. Hopkins (Maryknoll, NY: Orbis Books, 1999).
[15]Alistair Kee, *The Rise and Demise of Black Theology* (Aldershot, UK: Ashgate Publishing Limited, 2006), ix–x.

systemic problems within the movement. Instead the book simply restated many of the same antiquated formulas of the early 1970s about black victimology at the hands of whites.

Cone did, however, offer his latest assessment of the future of black liberation theology and vehemently maintained that black theology needs to continue to develop in the following ways: (1) develop an enduring radical race critique against white Christians; (2) broaden liberation themes to include gender, class, and sexuality; (3) incorporate material from slave narratives; and (4) conduct a critical rereading of the Bible in the light of the history and culture of black people.[16] However, Cone still argued that constructing a "truly radical race critique" should be the primary focus of black liberation theology.[17] Cone continued, "There can be no racial healing without dialogue, without ending the white silence on racism. . . . Racism is still with us in the academy, in the churches, and in every segment of the society."[18] He concluded that the challenge for black theology in the twenty-first century is to develop a penetrating race critique so that "no one will be able to forget the horrible crimes of white supremacy in the modern world."[19] Despite his passionate call, Cone's critique remains insufficient to revive black theology's usefulness for the black church because of its narrow scope regarding the realities of the black experience.

NEW CRITIQUES FOR BLACK THEOLOGY'S FUTURE FROM THE SECOND GENERATION: DWIGHT HOPKINS

Dwight Hopkins, a student of James Cone and slated as the heir apparent of the Conian vision, also critiques black theology by stressing a broader future than the standard corpus addresses.[20]

---

[16]James H. Cone, "Looking Back, Going Forward: Black Theology as Public Theology," in *Black Faith and Public Talk*, 255–256. See also Delores C. Carpenter, "A Time of Honor: A Portrait of African-American Clergywomen," *The Journal of Religious Thought* 56–57:2–1 (Spring-Fall 2000–2001): 75–94. See also Monica C. Jones, "The Spirit of Hagar: Living in an Unfriendly House," *Journal of the Interdenominational Theological Center* 31:1–2 (Fall/Spring 2003–2004): 61–83.

[17]Cone, "Looking Back, Going Forward," 256.

[18]Ibid.

[19]Ibid., 257.

[20]See also Matthew W. Hughey, "Moving Beyond 'Liberation Theology,'" *The Journal of Religious Thought* 57–58:2–2 (2005): 39–66.

Hopkins, carrying on the tradition of victimology, is concerned that black theology might lose its focus on the black poor.

Hopkins argues that the second generation of black liberation theologians must ask whether it has tried to work for the interests of the African-American poor. "'Liberation' defines black theology because the sacred spirit of God and black ancestors focus on the practice of freedom for the marginalized of all societies. Black theology must avoid omitting the crucial phrase of *liberation of the poor*. In ambiguity lies the danger."[21]

This disconnection from the ongoing victimology of the black poor, Hopkins fears, has led some black liberation scholars to jettison "the liberation of the poor" from black theological reflection. Not to keep the victimization of the black poor in the forefront seems egregious in Hopkins's view because of the "current state of structural poverty" in the black community.[22]

Hopkins also charges that many current black liberation theologians have lost their prophetic voice because their current positions on various faculties have created "historical amnesia," resulting in the overintellectualizing of theology that should be directed at meeting the needs of blacks who remain victims of poverty and white racism. Education has become the new villain because it has created a gap between black professors and the black church. The ivory tower is to blame for keeping black theologians away from the masses of poor blacks in America. Black intellectuals have lost the ability to communicate with the black poor, especially black women. Black women's victimology continues because of their "day-to-day triple experiences of economic dislocation, gender oppression, and racial negativities."[23]

In the end, Hopkins offers new vistas for black theology if it is to remain vibrant in its focus on the victims of oppression.[24] First, Hopkins offers a new commonwealth of economic redistribution.

---

[21]Dwight N. Hopkins, *Heart and Head: Black Theology—Past, Present, and Future* (New York: Palgrave, 2002), 162, italics his.
[22]Ibid.
[23]Ibid., 168.
[24]Ibid., 176–180. See also Linda E. Thompson, ed., *Living Stones in the Household of God* (Minneapolis: Fortress Press, 2004).

Black theology must promote a platform of economic socialism as it brings the reality of heaven to earth. Black theology will be effective when "all of the poor will start to share collectively in the vast resources offered by God to everyone."[25] Rich people are to be held accountable to a gospel that says, "Everyone ought to have equal stake at each level in society."[26] All of humanity is meant to share equally in the best of God's creation. In the best society, "no one human being will rule over another and no one individual or group of families will own more than anyone else."[27] There will be no victims of poverty because all of society will share the wealth of that society. Poverty will disappear for black victims, says Hopkins, when the poor share in the abundance of wealth and break the current global monopolization of the earth's resources, thereby bringing about a democracy, which requires "reallocation of current political economic structures toward sharing."[28]

Second, political leaders should be elected only from victimized communities. According to Hopkins, since the majority of the U.S. population is made up of poor and working people, the elected officials in local, state, and national levels should be from those groups as this guarantees true political democracy.[29]

Third, society should maintain a focus on racism. The African-American poor and working people need to be in a context where society celebrates the "richness of the racial characteristics" that God has given blacks. This should happen among blacks themselves, so that blacks, and others, can learn to love being black and blacks can "stop trying to imitate white people."[30]

Fourth, black women should assume more leadership roles. Poor black women who are victims of a tripartite oppressive context (race, gender, class) must be put in "leadership roles and make

---

[25]Hopkins, *Heart and Head*, 176.
[26]Ibid.
[27]Ibid., 178.
[28]Ibid., 179–180. For models of how black liberation models black church involvement in the economic spheres, see Marsha Snulligan Haney, "The Black Church: Missio Dei and Giving," *Journal of the Interdenominational Theological Center* 31:1–2 (Fall/Spring 2003–2004): 179–205.
[29]Hopkins, *Heart and Head*, 181.
[30]Ibid., 183. Also see Reginald F. Davis, "African-American Interpretation of Scripture," *The Journal of Religious Thought* 57–58:2–2 (2005): 93.

major decisions in every section of the nation—business ownership, politics, education, religion, the family, and more."[31] For example, since African-American women make up 70 percent of the congregations, then 70 percent of the black pastors should be women.[32]

Fifth, black liberation theologians should support gay and lesbian sexuality. Hopkins maintains that the tragedy of African-American heterosexuals is that they continue a system of oppression, using some of the same arguments that whites have used against blacks and that men have used against women, only for purposes of oppressing gay and lesbian sexuality. If passages in the Bible are objected to because they were wrongly used to justify slavery, then it stands to reason, in Hopkins's view, that the Bible remains questionable on homosexual practice. For Hopkins, divine love provides liberation for all humanity:

> If it is wrong to interpret the Hebrew story and the Jesus narratives as instructing black slaves to obey white masters and women to obey men, then why isn't it wrong to interpret this same Bible as saying homosexuals should deny the sexual orientation that God gave them when God created them?[33]

Sixth, attention must be given to children and the elderly. Liberation theology must engage the plights of child poverty and the growing needs of the elderly.[34]

---

[31]Hopkins, *Heart and Head*, 185. See also Judith Soares, "Gender Justice and the Christian Mission," *The Journal of Religious Thought* 57–58:2–2 (2005): 67–82 and Jacquelyn Grant, "Womanist Jesus and the Mutual Struggle for Liberation and on Containing God (Matthew 17:1–7 with Special Emphasis on Matthew 17:4)," *Journal of the Interdenominational Theological Center* 31:1–2 (Fall/Spring 2003–2004): 3–33.

[32]See also Paula L. McGee, "Divine Divas," *Journal of the Interdenominational Theological Center* 31:1–2 (Fall/Spring 2003–2004): 207–214 and Anne Streaty Wimberly and Elaine Crawford, "God's People, God's Earth Project: The Interrelated Oppression of Women and Nature," *Journal of the Interdenominational Theological Center* 31:1–2 (Fall/Spring 2003–2004): 215–241.

[33]Hopkins, *Heart and Head*, 187. Also see Kelly Douglas Brown and Ronald E. Hopson, "Understanding the Black Church: The Dynamics of Change," *The Journal of Religious Thought* 56–57:2–1 (Spring/Fall 2000–2001): 110.

[34]The Interdenominational Theological Center in Atlanta recently devoted an entire issue of their academic journal to children and youth. See also Marsha Snulligan Haney, "The Urban Child, Congregational Ministry and the Challenge of Religious Diversity," *Journal of the Interdenominational Theological Center* 30:1–2 (Fall/Spring 2002–2003): 9–36; Cheryl A. Kirk-Duggan, "I Cry for You," *Journal of the Interdenominational Theological Center* 30:1–2 (Fall/Spring 2002–2003): 37–38; Zvi Shapiro, "Children and the Seder," *Journal of the Interdenominational Theological Center* 30:1–2 (Fall/Spring 2002–2003): 39–62; Mark Ellingsen, "An Augustinian Approach to Parenting for the New Millennium," *Journal of the Interdenominational Theological Center* 30:1–2 (Fall/Spring 2002–2003): 65–76; Stephen C.

Seventh, an emphasis must be placed on emotional and psychological needs. The poor need action taken to restore their emotional centers that have been wounded by negative and traumatic experiences of the past.[35]

Eighth, Hopkins asserts that black theology needs to develop a theology of nature or ecology, not only because all people are contributing to the death of nature, but also because of environmental racism: "most dump sites in America are found in or very near black and Latino/Hispanic working-class populations."[36]

Lastly, there should be a concentration on the Third World. Black theology needs to increase its dialogue with other oppressed and victimized black poor and poor non-whites in Africa, Asia, the Caribbean, Latin America, the Pacific Islands, and North America. Hopkins is concerned that Christians, Muslims, Buddhists, African indigenous religions, Shintoists, Shamanists, Taoists, Confucianists, Jainists, Hindus, Jews, and others come together based on the belief in the practice of liberating victims from poverty and oppression.[37]

In sum, Hopkins's belief that victimology has not gone far enough judges the future of black liberation by a single test: "Do they side with God's work to liberate the poor and working-class people of all colors and ethnicities and bring in a new common wealth?"[38] Hopkins's new critiques, however, leave black theology

---

Rasor, "Our Children and Welfare" *Journal of the Interdenominational Theological Center* 30:1–2 (Fall/Spring 2002–2003): 77–92; Christine D. Chapman, "A Public Team Ministry for Teen Mothers and Their Babies," *Journal of the Interdenominational Theological Center* 30:1–2 (Fall/Spring 2002–2003): 93–108; Elizabeth J. Walker, "Pastoral Counseling with African-American Male Youth Offenders," *Journal of the Interdenominational Theological Center* 30:1–2 (Fall/Spring 2002–2003): 109–128; Bridgette Hector, "Womanist Model: Crossing Class Barriers: Middle Class Black Women Relating with Inner-City Black Female Youth," *Journal of the Interdenominational Theological Center* 30:1–2 (Fall/Spring 2002–2003): 129–145.

[35]See Carolyn Akua L. McCrary, "Intimate Violence against Black Women and Internalized Shame: A Womanist Pastoral Counseling Perspective," *Journal of the Interdenominational Theological Center* 28:1–2 (Fall/Spring 2000–2001): 3–38.

[36]Hopkins, *Heart and Head*, 190. See also Anthony B. Pinn, "Of God, Money, and Earth: The Black Church on Economics and Environmental Racism," *The Journal of Religious Thought* 56–57:2–1 (Spring-Fall 2001): 43–61.

[37]See also Richard Rose, "Howard Thurman on Religious Pluralism: Diversity in Harmony," *The Journal of Religious Thought* 55–56:2–1 (Spring-Fall 1999): 19–46 and Theodore Walker Jr., "The Black and Red: Responding to Sioux and Other Native American Instructions on Red-Black Solidarity," *The Journal of Religious Thought* 55–56:2–1 (Spring-Fall 1999): 73–86.

[38]Hopkins, *Heart and Head*, 192. See also Harold Dean Trulear, "Standing in the Gap: Pastoral Theology in the African-American Church," *The Journal of Religious Thought* 57–58:2–2 (2005): 19–37 and Rosetta E. Rose, "From Civil Rights to Civic Participation," *Journal of the Interdenominational Theological Center* 28:1–2 (Fall-Spring 2000–2001): 39–77.

in the same useless spot, because it continues to ground theology in a black consciousness construed as "victim."

A BLACK EVANGELICAL CRITIQUE: BRUCE FIELDS

Bruce Fields offers five cogent ways in which black theology must jettison its experience-oriented approach and exchange it for thoroughly orthodox categories and orientations. Fields provides an assessment that addresses some of the implications of developing theology without presupposing the triune God and the authority of Scripture.

First, Fields maintains that grounding theology in human experience alone introduces a kind of divergence from the intent of the biblical story. Fields notes, "Experience, apart from the transcendent perspective of revelation as embodied in Scripture and practiced in the community yielded to Scripture, cannot be evaluated."[39] Therefore, black liberation theology becomes no more than a competition with other "oppressed" groups to determine who is the loudest or the most persuasive, rhetorically speaking, in order to determine what shape the Christian life should take for blacks (and other oppressed groups). In the end, Fields suggests that black theology can degenerate into sociology that is "merely baptized with Christian terminology."[40] Using experience as a theological starting point also wrongly forsakes Christian foundations as seen, for example, in the work of recent black religious scholars like Anthony Pinn. Pinn argues that African-Americans need to question not only the existence of God but also the need for a theology of liberation altogether because human liberation matters more than theism.[41]

Second, Fields reminds black liberation theologians that a theology of victimology does not prevent black theology from locating itself within the tradition of the Christian church. Citing the bad practices of past generations of Christians, including slave owner-

---

[39]Bruce Fields, *Introducing Black Theology: Three Crucial Questions for the Evangelical Church* (Grand Rapids, MI: Baker Academic, 2001), 73.
[40]Ibid.
[41]Ibid. See also Anthony B. Pinn, *Why Lord? Suffering and Evil in Black Theology* (New York: Continuum, 1995).

ship, racism, oppression, Eurocentrism, and the like, is insufficient ground to attempt to dislocate black theology from a theological emphasis derived from the biblical and theological tradition of orthodox Christianity. Fields explains:

> There is a network of beliefs that makes a church Christian as opposed to other religious forms or types of sociocultural institutions. The misapplication of a doctrine does not, in and of itself, make the doctrine untrue, Eurocentric, or enslaving. The church, black or white, is the church because of adherence to certain truths correctly held as transcendent, normative, and authoritative. Such a belief system inherently encompasses beliefs about the nature of God, Scripture, Jesus Christ, humanity, and the Holy Spirit.[42]

Third, Fields believes that black theology needs to adopt different systems of hermeneutics. The hermeneutic of victimology, based on deconstruction, oppression, and sociocritical approaches to Scripture, steer black theology farther and farther away from the theology of the Bible. Moreover, black theological hermeneutics oriented exclusively around the black experience keeps black theology from connecting to the rest of the Christian church and impedes reconciliation with various nonblack communities within the church.[43]

Fourth, black theology cannot exist without the larger (white) theological community. Fields correctly points out that most black liberation theologians were trained at predominantly white theological institutions and primarily read the theology of western (liberal) theologians and philosophers, which makes a clean break from white theologians impossible.

White Europeans are significant contributors to Western Christianity in all of its forms, even in black churches, and Fields raises two important questions for black liberation theologians to address. First, is it possible for black theologians to be free from the restraints of the dominant theological culture? Second, if white theology is to be rejected, how can black theologians effect change in the theology and sociocultural attitudes of the dominant cul-

---

[42]Fields, *Introducing Black Theology*, 77–78.
[43]Ibid., 81.

ture? These questions point out the severe limitations of attempts to develop a distinctively racially contrived theology built from the history of the church. Fields warns, "Serious challenges to and reformulation of core beliefs will position black theology away from orthodox faith, inhibiting its contribution to the African-American church and community and eventually ushering it into nonexistence."[44]

Fifth, Fields proposes that black theology is in danger of losing a distinctively Christian identity in several areas:[45] (1) Black theologians maintain that God is a God of liberation from social oppression while the Scriptures portray a God who is also a God who demands obedience and makes provision for his own so they are equipped to obey. Human incapacity was factored into the covenantal and redemptive framework of the biblical story, calling for radical transformation of God's people. (2) The atonement needs to be recovered in its historic definition. Womanist theologians, for example, argue that the cross does not represent substitutionary atonement but rather represents the evil response of human principalities and powers to Jesus who came to demonstrate an example of how to live a holistic life.[46] In general, black liberation theologians only offer a sociocultural interpretation of the atonement.[47] Fields is quick to point out that while the atonement does have social implications, Christ's work on the cross is a manifestation of power and is the source for the hope of overcoming all sins in human life, personal and social alike. (3) Black theology needs a biblical anthropology. In contrast to the sociopragmatic approach of black liberation theology, which defines the *imago Dei* in terms of race, class, gender, and sexual orientation, a distinctively biblical approach recognizes the innate equality of human ontology in terms of human dignity. It is grounded in its deepest form in Genesis 1:26–28 instead of in Marxist categories. Fields is cor-

---

[44]Ibid., 85.
[45]Ibid., 91–105.
[46]Ibid., 92. See also Delores S. Williams, *Sisters in the Wilderness* (Maryknoll, NY: Orbis, 1993), 60–61.
[47]See Evans Jr., *We Have Been Believers: An African-American Systematic Theology*, 77–98.

rect to highlight that men and women are defined in relationship to God and his will as revealed in Scripture.[48] (4) Black liberation theology needs to recover the doctrine of salvation. Black liberation theology places such an overwhelming emphasis on the analysis of human oppression and the liberation of the oppressed that issues of what is required for an individual to be reconciled to God either go unanswered or are redefined in terms of social activism. Namely, either being oppressed or advocating for the oppressed seems to be all that is required, which contradicts the plain teaching of Scripture in several places.

Until black liberation theology recovers the good and right aspects of orthodox Christian theology, it will remain nothing more than sociopragmatism sprinkled with Christian language. In fact, Alistair Kee argues that black theology is dead because it has become nothing more than sociology and must be completely reconstituted if it is ever to make a positive contribution to the Christianity of blacks or to the church at large.

THE DEMISE OF BLACK LIBERATION THEOLOGY: ALISTAIR KEE

Alistair Kee, professor emeritus of theology at the University of Edinburgh, recently published a devastating blow to black theology that warrants significant discussion, even beyond the scope of this book. Kee gives black liberation theology an F because it has failed to speak to core structural issues facing today's black poor and has failed to speak to the completely changed social, political, and economic realities of blacks in America. Kee believes that blacks who live below the poverty line are poor for reasons other than racially reasoned ones. In fact, Kee views the plight of the black poor in terms of economic bifurcations, not racial variance. He writes, "In the present context the issue is the suffering of poor black people which no longer arises predominantly from race but from the inherent inequities of American capitalism."[49]

---

[48]Fields, *Introducing Black Theology*, 100.
[49]Kee, *The Rise and Demise of Black Theology*, ix.

According to Kee, in 2006 blacks were no longer victims of oppressive American life but "beneficiaries. The rising black middle class has done very well in recent years."[50] Blacks in America are no longer victims because they now assume a commonality of interest with whites when U.S. companies strike deals with corrupt foreign regimes or decimate the environment of desperately poor communities. Kee goes on to argue that as American citizens, voters, and consumers, blacks should be able to have more influence in American policies toward Africa.

Kee believes that American black liberation theology has no future because it has failed to respond to the new realities of the black community and society in general, especially as it relates to class. The notion of "blackness," Kee maintains, is actually not determined by blacks but by whites.

> The content of being black, the features that it is claimed are determined are not constructed by whim or whimsy but according to the political interests of those who hold and exercise power . . . those [who are] mainly white. It has proved notoriously difficult for black writers to define what they mean by the category.[51]

Being black also is not a self-defining natural state. Defining blackness is not just a social construct, affected by whites, but it seems that initially the definition of black is simply "not-white."[52] This calls into question if the term *black* in *black theology* is useful at all.

Black is not a natural or neutral term, but a historically rooted political and social construct, Kee argues. The term *black* may be a form of self-abuse because it is difficult to imagine how the interests of white oppressors could be better served than by blacks accepting politically and socially contrived derogatory language.[53] Race has been used as a convenient red herring. Race is not so much about race, exclusively, as it is a term used in political spheres for those who construct negative images of social groups they seek to oppress

---

[50]Ibid. Also Earl D. Trent, "Breaking the Myths, Shattering the Shackles: Interpreting the Second Commandment," *The Journal of Religious Thought* 56–57:2–1 (Spring-Fall 2000–2001): 71–72.
[51]Kee, *The Rise and Demise of Black Theology*, 171.
[52]Ibid.
[53]Ibid., 172.

or manipulate. Kee maintains, in contradistinction to Cone, that race is not an ontological category and never will be.[54] Locating blackness in ontology handicaps black theology and locks blacks into nontranscendental racial reasoning that is unable to adapt and speak to the ever-changing socioeconomic diversities within black communities. In this sense, blackness is always defined in relationship to a permanent class of "white" adversaries determined to make blacks victims of oppression. It encourages a paranoid state where blacks are conditioned to always expect the worst from whites. The reduction of the black experience as victim, in the end, requires perpetual "whiteness" as a norm for understanding what it means to be black.

Cone and other early black theologians attempted to distance themselves from "white theology" by turning to black sources, grounded in the black experience in America, without any critical antithesis between those views and Christian theism. This subsequently opened the door for Cone's and West's embracing of Marxism, even with its atheist presuppositions, womanist theologians' use of the writings of Alice Walker, various black liberation theologians appealing to the pagan religious traditions of Africa, and black theology devolving into religious studies instead of theology.[55]

Again, one of Kee's primary critiques is that black theology fails to address the issues of class that are far more pervasive than race because of the new realities of this era. Racial discrimination and racial oppression are not the conditions that poor blacks find themselves in today. As long as black liberation theologians base their theology on the racial oppression of blacks, it will become more and more useless.

> By restricting their criticism to racial discrimination, black intellectuals focus on the symptoms of a sickness within American society, but fail to relate these to the dynamics of capitalism, to

---

[54]Ibid., 173.
[55]See, for example, Anthony B. Pinn, *Terror and Triumph: The Nature of Black Religion* (Minneapolis: Fortress Press, 2003).

the disparity of power, the maldistribution of wealth, oppressive relations of production and economic insecurity.[56]

Kee believes that the Marxism of Cornel West provides one of the most tragic missed opportunities for black theology to meet the challenges of a new era. Kee simply seems to want black liberation theology to transition from using race as a theological category to using class (in a Marxist sense), which, as we saw in a previous chapter, is equally destructive and contrary to the teachings of Scripture. Kee's primary weakness here is that he fails to see that adopting class categories is no better than adopting racial ones, leaving black theology no more useful to poor blacks. Reducing human anthropology to "victim" by virtue of economic status perpetuates the presuppositional problem. Kee sees that poverty is "produced by capitalism" and inaccurately interprets the ineffectiveness of black theology's future along those lines.[57] As we shall see later, the problems affecting black theology are more complex than a lack of Marxist class analysis.

Kee also notes that black liberation theology remains locked in the past. Now occupying many university posts, the second generation of black theologians employs a methodology that shackles black thought to historical sources, doing nothing more than regurgitating past formulas and critiques. Returning to historical sources, argues Kee, leads to neither original nor progressive writing in black theology.[58] The irony of the black theological method as it appeals to the authority of experience, oppression, and so on is that in doing so it has even more completely embraced European intellectual and cultural traditions.

Another glaring weakness of black theology locking into the past is historicism. Kee cites multiple examples involving Victor Anderson, who makes note of the second generation's historicist proclivity to reinterpret slave religion, using much Christian/African

---

[56]Kee, *The Rise and Demise of Black Theology,* 177.
[57]For a current assessment of trends in black urban church life, see Sandra Barnes, "Then and Now: A Comparative Analysis of the Urban Black Church in America," *Journal of the Interdenominational Theological Center* 29:1–2 (Fall-Spring 2001–2002): 137–156.
[58]Kee, *The Rise and Demise of Black Theology,* 182.

religious syncretism, as somehow a precursor of black theology. Anderson notes:

> [Black theology's] hermeneutics of narrative return ends up justifying the black theology project by a vicious circularity of reasoning that renders the legitimacy of slave religion coterminous with black theology and the legitimacy of black liberation theology conterminous with slave religion.[59]

Black liberation theology, by adopting a historicist approach, selects convenient dimensions of slave and African religion without a necessary biblical antithesis. Making slave religion conterminous with black liberation theology orients black theology toward the past exclusively with a concomitant tendency to define the future of blacks in America in terms of an identity derived from slavery alone.[60]

Kee is also quick to point out that the liberation motif is biblically flawed because "God is not represented in the Bible as one who releases slaves."[61] In fact, the word "slave," as presented in the biblical story, is not directly analogous to the black experience in America, which may explain Scripture's silence rather than outright condemnation of certain forms of slavery.[62] Based on recent history of Africans oppressing other Africans and the corporate silence on Africa in Conian black liberation theology, Kee concludes, "The representation of God as a God who releases captives [has] no basis in history."[63] Kee refers to the second generation of black theology shackled into interpreting a God who exclusively deals with racial victimology as "tired, over used and lacking in credibility."[64]

In the final analysis, Kee announces, "Black theology is dead."[65] Black theology is dead because the second generation is

---

[59]Victor Anderson, as quoted in ibid., 184.
[60]See Dwight N. Hopkins, *Down, Up, and Over: Slave Religion and Black Theology* (Minneapolis: Fortress Press, 2000).
[61]Kee, *The Rise and Demise of Black Theology*, 186.
[62]See J. Albert Harrill, *Slaves in the New Testament: Literary, Social, and Moral Dimensions* (Minneapolis: Fortress Press, 2006).
[63]Kee, *The Rise and Demise of Black Theology*, 186.
[64]Ibid.
[65]Ibid., 190.

doing nothing more than rearticulating the same cultural critique of thirty years ago, as if human progress ceased in the early 1970s. In the spirit of Cornel West, one might conclude that black theology rhetoric has become a substitute for analysis, loquacious tautologies have replaced serious scholarship, and uncreative thinking has led to rigor mortis.[66] Black liberation theology has failed to reach the black masses and remains primarily a theological playground for the black academic elite at select seminaries and departments of religion. Black liberation theology still remains inaccessible to most African-American Christians, and it has little to no global interest or influence.[67]

In conclusion, Kee offers this obituary to black theology:

> There is the arrogance of Black theology repeating year after year the same essentialisms and stereotypes which are frankly embarrassingly naïve in academic circles. There is a need for proper analysis of the worsening situation of black poverty, a little more humility in view of the fact that "we are more confused than ever about the reasons for it" . . . the forces of oppression and exploitation are increasingly taking control of the world through the processes of global capitalism. They cannot be successfully opposed simply by progressive Europeans. . . . Black Americans could play a vital part, if they read the new context and move their agenda forward.[68]

Even with Kee's alarmist and Marxist critiques, having raised several good points about black theologians needing to address current realities of the black poor and the Scriptures not defining God's mighty acts as being focused on freeing slaves, they remain insufficient to address the true cause of the death of black liberation theology: its misguided presuppositions. We now turn our attention to what is necessary for black theology to be resurrected as a theol-

---

[66]Ibid., 195. See also Cornel West, *Race Matters* (Boston: Beacon Press, 1993), 43.
[67]See Michael I. N. Dash, "African-American Congregational Life," *Journal of the Interdenominational Theological Center* 28:1–2 (Fall-Spring 2000–2001): 157–176 and Tamelyn Tucker-Worgs, "Get on Board, Little Children, There's Room for Many More: The Black Megachurch Phenomenon," *Journal of the Interdenominational Theological Center* 28:1–2 (Fall-Spring 2000–2001): 177–203.
[68]Kee, *The Rise and Demise of Black Theology*, 200.

ogy that is faithful both to the Scriptures and to the needs of black communities and churches.

ESSENTIAL PRESUPPOSITIONS FOR A NEW BLACK THEOLOGY

The above critiques of black liberation theology provide helpful insights into the internal limits of a theological system with starting points that set it up for extinction. Many of the current new critiques remain limited because they (with the exception of Fields's) fail to address core problems of fidelity to the presuppositions of Scripture and to redemptive history. What follows are the needed areas to reconstruct a theology that is not grounded in a victimized black identity but is grounded in the necessary trajectory of God's redemptive mission.

The Absolute Triune God as the Starting Point

As Roberts predicted in the early 1970s, the Barthian orientation of black liberation theology caused it to veer off course and landed it in the grave. At first glance, the Jesus talk of liberation theologians gives the appearance of fidelity to the triune God as attested in the Scriptures by the Holy Spirit. Additionally, the Barthian Christocentric emphasis of Jesus as the revelation of God, found in Cone and later in Hopkins, gives the appearance of good biblical theology. A closer look, however, reveals, like much of nineteenth- and twentieth-century theological liberalism, that black liberation theologians are redefining the knowledge of God as revealed in the whole of Scripture. We need not turn any further than to J. Gresham Machen to identify where black liberation theology went wrong in its development of the doctrine of the God of the oppressed while following the Barthian path set by James Cone.

While it is true that one can come to know God through Jesus, Machen points out, "Jesus plainly recognized the validity of other ways of knowing God, and to reject those other ways is to reject the things that lay at the very centre of Jesus' life."[69] These other ways, according to Machen, include nature, the moral law, and God as revealed in the Scriptures. The rejection of the authority of biblical revelation contributed to black theology's demise. Unless there is some understanding of the triune God, a God independent of Jesus, the ascription of deity to Jesus has no meaning.[70] Machen argues, "Jesus plainly found God revealed in the Scriptures."[71] The Incarnation revealed, in a most profound, dramatic, and intimate way, the character and nature of God, so much so that Machen maintains that such revelation obtained its true force and power only on the basis of the biblical story—namely, on the basis of both the Old Testament and Jesus' own teaching.

Christian theism is required if black theology is to develop any sort of theology that is faithful to the Scriptures and helpful to black communities—a Christian theism that knows God within the persons of the Trinity. Black liberation theologians would object to any notion of theism because it rightly restricts the implications of redemption to scriptural intent. The very basis of the religion of Jesus was a radical belief in the existence of a personal God as revealed in the Scriptures. Jesus' theism was not confined to the experience of social oppression or economic or political status, because his teaching presupposed a knowable and discernible God as revealed in the testimony of "the Law of Moses and the Prophets."[72] There can be no development of theology without understanding the authority of Scripture and the content therein—a personal triune God revealed in the redemptive biblical story.

Black liberation theology created a God who functions to liberate oppressed people from structures but who is not personal or demanding complete allegiance and fidelity. The absolute sovereignty and transcendence of the triune God as revealed in the Scriptures redirects the attention from a God only known through the lens of human experience to a God Creator whose priority is

---

[69] J. Gresham Machen, *Christianity and Liberalism* (Grand Rapids, MI: Eerdmans, 1999), 55.
[70] Ibid., 55–56.
[71] Ibid.
[72] Luke 24:44.

restoration of all creation. Black liberation theology blurs the distinction between God the Creator and mankind the creature, such that God's mission is reinterpreted through human experience. God exists, then, for human liberation as if he became God only after the insurgence of socio-political oppression into the human story. Black theology is in need of a robust doctrine of the triune God developed within a context of Christian theism.

The Absolute Primacy of Biblical Authority

In order to understand the needs of the black community and the black church, if black theology ever intends to have any actual impact by addressing issues related to the kingdom, accepting and endorsing the primacy of the Scriptures as authoritative revelation is paramount. The actual teaching of the Bible must be the focal point and starting point for all theological development.[73] The understanding and intelligibility of anything theologically related to the black experience must presuppose the existence of God, whose nature and character are delineated and attested in the Scriptures of both the Old and New Testaments.[74] The Scriptures are not simply one important source among others. They remain the ultimate and final authority for developing a theology that adequately interprets and effectively applies the redemptive story to the black experience.

We find in much of black liberation theology positions that are founded on shifting emotions and humanistic philosophies imposing positions onto the biblical story rather than deriving a theology from the redemptive story, self-attested by God. When the human authorities of the black experience replaced the self-authenticating authority of the Scriptures, as Kee's obituary articulated, black liberation theology died. Essentially, black liberation theology was dead from the beginning. Redefining God in terms of oppression and reorienting the redemptive story around the liberation of people under socioeconomic and political oppression, Cone increasingly thwarted the authority of Scripture and traded it for black power,

---

[73]Greg L. Bahnsen, *Van Til's Apologetics* (Phillipsburg, NJ: P&R, 1998), 198.
[74]Cornelius Van Til, *The Reformed Pastor and Modern Thought* (Phillipsburg, NJ: P&R, 1980), 12.

Marxism, cultural relativism, and the like. What black theology must do is believe God at his word, on the basis of his authority, and renounce autonomous wisdom.[75] To that end, Bavinck notes:

> As the word of God [the Bible] stands of high level above all human authority in state and society, science and art. Before it, all else must yield. For people must obey God rather than people. All other [human] authority is restricted to its own circle and applies only to its own area. But the authority of Scripture extends to the whole person and over all humankind. It is above the intellect and the will, the heart and the conscience, and cannot be compared with any other authority. Its authority, being divine, is absolute.[76]

It is the primacy of biblical authority that provides the right platform for understanding contextualization, as discussed in the previous chapter. Genuine black theology cannot exist without the biblical witness as the final authority.

Human Dignity Grounded in *Imago Dei* (Instead of Race)

Black theology must focus on the human dignity of all races, a dignity that is grounded in the *imago Dei*. The human person we are told about in the biblical story is made in the image and likeness of God and is given a calling. This arrangement comes with certain implications, rights, and responsibilities that are essential for black theology to communicate to people who are poor (and everyone else for that matter). The implications of the *imago Dei* as described in the Scriptures are the scaffolding through which injustice is defined and human life has meaning here and now.

Gerard Van Groningen offers a concise presentation of man and woman that will be helpful here. Biblical passages such as Genesis 1:26–30 and 2:7–25 paint a clear picture of what those bearing the image of God were designed to do. Van Groningen maintains that God planned the creation of man and woman. He had a pre-

---

[75]Herman Bavinck, *Reformed Dogmatics, Volume 1: Prolegomena*, trans. John Vriend, ed. John Bolt (Grand Rapids, MI: Baker Academic, 2003), 464.
[76]Ibid., 165.

determined purpose for humanity to cocreate with God.[77] Man and woman were to be rulers over the natural creation, to have a superior role, a dominant influence, and a responsible service. Man and woman were to be royal representatives within the cosmic kingdom. Their relationship to the cosmic kingdom was one of inherent integrality.

The human person is part of creation and is involved in its continued existence, development, and beautification. Van Groningen refers to four central implications of what it means to be made in the image and likeness of God.[78] First, as an image bearer, the human person is to mirror God, thinking God's thoughts after him, representing God. Since God is a personal being, to be a person is to know the good, to have a conscience, a sense of privilege and responsibility. Second, as God is spirit, the human person is a spiritual personality. Each person has the capacity to commune intimately with God, to know him, to trust, love, desire, and obey him. Third, as God has the capacity to execute his will and purposes to achieve his goals, God has endowed human persons with a capacity to use that which God has provided to give expression to their personality, spirituality, and virtues. Lastly, God is relational, and by extension the human person is charged with living in relationship with God and others.

With these attributes, man and woman were given a cultural mandate to exercise their role as vicegerents by ruling over, developing, and simultaneously maintaining the cosmos. Man and woman were given a social mandate that involves their roles as parents and the establishment of family and community. So being made in God's image entails freedom and the capacity to think, create, produce, cultivate, make choices and decisions without being forced, and enjoy beautiful things. We rest, we embrace lives of activity, we have deep personal relationships with God and others, we desire physical intimacy, we need community, and so on.

---

[77]Gerard Van Groningen, *From Creation to Consummation* (Sioux Center, IA: Dordt College Press, 1997), 53–79.
[78]Ibid., 63.

If we recognize that we all share the same dignity and bear the same image, it follows that everyone deserves certain treatment.[79] The human person is created to enjoy fellowship with God and other persons and to rule over nature; these attributes should be encouraged for all—not promoted for some and withheld from others. The oppressors and the oppressed have the same inherent dignity, and both should be called to lives that reflect the original design of God for humanity (Rom. 8:29; Col. 3:9–11). What black liberation theologians must communicate to their constituents is what God has attested to regarding the implications for true humanity. To communicate these truths is to instill the type of dignity that truly invites people to have lives that are in harmony with God's intentions for human life.

Rediscovering a Biblical Doctrine of Sin: Personal and Social

As mentioned previously, sin must be explicated both in its personal and structural dimensions. The biblical story records a history of sin that includes dimensions of both personal sin and structural sin.

Personal sin. The entrance of depravity into the world, as the consequence of the Fall (Gen 3:1–13), greatly affected man's ability to function as the person originally designed and created to exhibit the attributes of the Creator. In fact, the image was impaired, affecting everything, including man's ability to think correctly about the world. Not only are humans morally and intellectually limited, but also—because of the implications of the Fall—human nature is predisposed toward things unintended by the Creator.

This sinfulness not only entered the human hearts of all those descended from Adam but also cursed the state of nature (Gen. 3:14–19). Original sin passed to all humans and characterizes all of us to the same extent.[80] It affected man's ability to do good and

---

[79]Samuel Gregg, *Economic Thinking for the Theologically Minded* (Lanham, MD: University Press of America, 2001), 4.
[80]Herman Bavinck, *Reformed Dogmatics, Volume 3: Sin and Salvation*, trans John Vriend, ed. John Bolt (Grand Rapids, MI: Baker Academic, 2006), 127.

think analogously with God. The pervasiveness of sin has also created a context in which the cosmos is cursed, not functioning as it was originally designed to function, including the *telos* of humanity to glorify God. Combining human sinfulness with the overall fall of the created order has led to every form of injustice and error imaginable (Rom. 1:21, 28–32).

Consistent with the *imago Dei*, Bavinck maintains that even though the human person is fallen, he maintains all his "components, capacities, and power, the form, the character and nature, [but] the set and direction of all these capacities, and powers were so changed that now, instead of fulfilling the will of God, they fulfill the 'law of the flesh.'"[81]

Abraham Kuyper describes the reality of this world by highlighting two deleterious post-Fall attributes of man that he calls *error* and *sin*:

> *Error* insofar as there was ignorance about the essence of man and his social attributes, as well as about the laws that govern human association and the production, distribution, and use of material goods. *Sin* insofar as greed and lust for power (expressed either through force or through vicious custom and unjust law) disturbed or checked the healthy growth of human society, sometimes cultivating a very cancerous development for centuries. In time, both sin and error joined forces to enthrone false principles that violated human nature.[82]

In other words, the sinfulness of man, combined with the noetic effects of sin, opened human reasoning to error, and this has led to much injustice and has retarded the social and economic development of many countries. Because of the state of sin in creation, human persons are prone to think incorrectly about God and about societal and economic relationships. The ultimate causes of social and economic injustice in the world reside in the realm of the Enemy, who works through the sins and errors

---

[81]Ibid., 140.
[82]Abraham Kuyper, *The Problem of Poverty*, ed. James W. Skillen (Grand Rapids, MI: Baker Books, 1991), 31, italics his.

of fallen human beings (John 8:44; Acts 13:10; Rev. 12:9). The combination of sinfulness and error provides the platform for structural sin.

Structural sin. George Yancey highlights the fact that structural sin operates freely in our society and impacts the life of every minority.[83] Structural sins impacting blacks in America were born out of historical injustices that formed a society in which discrimination is a natural part, whether individual members are racist or not.[84] For blacks, these structural forms of racism are found in residential segregation and in education institutions of white preference, Yancey argues.[85] Fields applauds black theology on this point, noting that "as a movement [black theology] reminds the church of the pervasiveness of sin in systems, structures, and sociopolitical institutions."[86]

Systemic and structural sins result in the perpetuation of "injustice to, and dehumanization of, select groups in sociocultural constructs."[87] As such, institutional racism emerged after the civil rights movement as the next great evil to be tackled. Structural and institutional racism permits whites to maintain control over blacks and must be eliminated in order to achieve true racial harmony in all sectors of society.[88] As stated earlier, Fields believes that evangelicals tend toward more privatized dispositions and are suspicious of addressing structural issues for three reasons: (1) Sociopolitical involvement may undermine orthodox doctrine; (2) some eschatological positions cause Christians to withdraw from culture and have a pessimistic attitude toward human culture and social involvement; and (3) our individualistic tendencies draw us away from a community consciousness that would aid us

---

[83]George A. Yancey, *Beyond Black and White: Reflections on Racial Reconciliation* (Grand Rapids, MI: Baker Books, 1996), 43.
[84]Ibid.
[85]Ibid., 43–47.
[86]Fields, *Introducing Black Theology*, 67.
[87]Ibid., 68.
[88]Mid-Peninsula Christian Ministry, "Institutional Racism in American Society," in *Moral Issues and Christian Response*, ed. Paul T. Jersild and Dale A. Johnson (New York: Holt, Rinehart, and Winston, 1971), 254–268.

in caring and identifying systemic and structural sin "because it gets our eyes off of ourselves."[89]

Cornel West maintains that black theology has not gone far enough in addressing structural sin. Early conceptions of black theology, according to West, had severe limitations in this area. West understands the early limitations of black theology dealing structurally in its

> absence of a systematic social analysis, which has prevented black theologians from coming to terms with the relationships between racism, sexism, class exploitation and imperialist oppression . . . [and] its tendency to downplay existential issues such as death, disease, dread, despair and disappointment which are related to yet not identical with suffering caused by oppressive social structures.[90]

American society continues to be a place rife with racist structures.[91] Blacks continue to be victims of racist structures in the areas of banking, mortgage appropriations, disability benefits, small business loans, underfunded black schools, and so on.[92] West, in the end, finds himself in the same victimologist quicksand that caused the original demise of black liberation theology.

With a correctly biblical understanding of sin in its personal and structural dimensions, black theology will be able to develop an ecclesiology that fits with the Scripture's witness to the work and person of Christ as well as appropriating a sound articulation of social justice. The doctrines of Christology and ecclesiology are inseparably tied to Scripture's attestation of all forms of sin and God's means of addressing it. Black theology will remain useless to the black church and to black communities unless it embraces biblical teachings on the fact and implications of the Fall.

---

[89]Fields, *Introducing Black Theology*, 69.
[90]Cornel West, "Black Theology of Liberation as Critique of Capitalist Civilization," in *Black Theology: A Documentary History, Volume II: 1980–1992*, ed. James H. Cone and Gayraud S. Wilmore (Maryknoll, NY: Orbis Books, 1993), 416.
[91]Sharon D. Welch, *Reconstructing Christian Theology* (Minneapolis: Fortress Press, 1994), 173–174.
[92]Ibid.

Justice in Line with the Redemptive Mission of God

With James Cone's and Cornel West's introduction of Marxism as the vision for an ethical framework for the black church, black liberation theology experienced an ever-greater separation from the Scriptures as well as from the mainstream black church. Any conception of justice must be formulated in conjunction with the redemptive mission of God as revealed in the Scriptures. If black theology is to benefit the church at all, its concept of justice must be shaped presupposing the Scriptures rather than adopting an atheistic ethic grounded in emotional rhetoric and pragmatism.

Conceptions of justice in line with redemptive history demonstrate God's intention for human life and creation. David Jones defines justice in this way: "Justice means that every human being should be treated according to what it means to be human, and what it means to be human is to be one who bears the image of God and who has a divine calling to fulfill."[93] This concept of justice is drawn from the Scripture's teaching regarding the redemptive mission of God. Since God is personal and conscious, every mode of his self-disclosure is a faultless expression of his nature and purpose for human life.[94] As Gerhardus Vos maintains, "The presupposition of all knowledge of God is man's having been created in the image of God."[95] As such, what God intends for the *imago Dei* in redemptive history becomes paramount in understanding the concept of justice.

Within the context of redemptive history, the Scriptures call God's people to be visible to the nations as salt and light by the quality of their moral lives in order that their ethical visibility will ultimately bring the nations to glorify God.[96] Bringing glory to God in redemptive history is a call both to evangelism and to social action. Black liberation theology failed to emphasize one and overemphasized the other. Social action and evangelism are works of the church in the world. But social justice issues, while vital, do

---

[93]David Clyde Jones, *Biblical Christian Ethics* (Grand Rapids, MI: Baker Books, 1994), 83.
[94]Gerhardus Vos, *Biblical Theology* (Edinburgh: The Banner of Truth Trust, 1996), 11.
[95]Ibid., 19.
[96]Christopher J. H. Wright, *The Mission of God: Unlocking the Bible's Grand Narrative* (Downers Grove, IL: InterVarsity Press, 2006), 389.

not constitute the totality of what God intends for a covenant relationship with his people and his world.[97] Simply affecting social or economic contexts does not address issues of sin or the call for all to unite in the work and person of Christ. On the other hand, dismissing the redemptive witness of the kingdom in the church's social action runs the risk of denying God's people opportunities to love their neighbors, live as salt and light, bring the kingdom to bear in all spheres of life, and be a blessing to the nations (Gen. 18:18–19). Wright notes:

> Spiritual evangelism means that the gospel is presented only as a means of having your own sins forgiven and having assurance of a future with God in heaven—without either the moral challenge of walking with personal integrity in the world of social, economic and political society around us, or the missional challenge of being actively concerned for issues of justice and compassion for others. The result is a kind of privatized pietism, or one that is cosily shared with like-minded believers but has little cutting edge or prophetic relevance in the relation to wider society.[98]

This is important because James Cone first wrote out of frustration that white Christians were not talking about issues of justice during the civil rights movement. One can only wonder if black liberation theology after Cone would have even developed had Cone's theological community been actively bringing the redemptive imperatives of the kingdom to bear on racial issues in America during the civil rights movement. With these issues in mind, it is not an exaggeration to conclude that redemptive mission without social compassion and justice is biblically deficient.[99]

For black theology to embrace justice in light of the ongoing redemptive mission of God, the focus must again return to seeking to render impartially to everyone his or her due in proper proportion according to the norm of God's intentions for men and women made in his image, regardless of race.[100] Impartial justice does not

---

[97]Ibid., 287.
[98]Ibid.
[99]Ibid., 288.
[100]See E. Calvin Beisner, "Justice and Poverty: Two Views Contrasted," in *Christianity and*

detest all things white or black nor embrace group (racial) favoritism. Instead justice demands that special attention be paid to the weak members of society while requiring conditions such that each person is able to participate in society in a way compatible with human dignity.[101] It is the revelation of Scripture that provides both broad and narrow parameters for justice.

Justice does not exist in the abstract as nothing more than a guide for the cultural life of the church. On the contrary, biblical justice in harmony with the redemptive story has a *telos*: the mission of God to redeem the whole creation ignited by the love of God. Charles Hodge writes, "The blessedness of the redeemed will flow not only from the manifestation of the glory [of God], but also of the love of God; of that love, mysterious, unchangeable, and infinite, of which the work of redemption is the fruit."[102]

The fruits of redemption are revealed not only in Scripture but also through God's people, the church, practicing justice before the nations, bringing God's norms to bear in every area of human activity.

In sum, the passion for justice must be grounded in the final authority of Scripture for black theology since it is from God that we derive our passion for justice and liberation according to what has been revealed about the God who battles injustice, oppression, and bondage throughout history right to the Eschaton.[103] All true liberation, biblically speaking, flows from the sovereign God of redemptive history, incarnate in Jesus Christ, so that humanity and creation conform to the will and glory of God revealed in the Scriptures.

CONCLUSION

As Alistair Kee pronounced, black liberation theology is dead. Black liberation theology was doomed from the beginning because its ini-

Economics in the Post-Cold War Era: The Oxford Declaration and Beyond, ed. Herbert Schlossberg, Vinay Samuel, and Ronald Sider (Grand Rapids, MI: Eerdmans, 1994), 64–65.
[101]"The Oxford Declaration," in ibid., 22–23.
[102]Charles Hodge, *Systematic Theology*, Vol. III (Grand Rapids, MI: Eerdmans, 1997), 860.
[103]Wright, *The Mission of God*, 44.

tial biblical and theological presuppositions were grounded in the black experience in America as "victim." Early in the development of black liberation theology, J. Deotis Roberts clearly pointed out core weaknesses but, like most other critics, simply did not go deep enough to the level of presupposition. In order for any black theology to help the black church, it must be formulated with a foundation of biblically constrained presuppositions. Contextualizing the redemptive story in the black experience, then, can be done with the strictest fidelity to the will of God for human persons and creation, personally and structurally, as revealed in the Scriptures. Black theology has a future only if it presupposes the self-attestation of the triune God and seeks to interpret the black experience through the lens of the entirety of Scripture, pursuing both justice and mercy (Mic. 6:8).

Further Reading

BLACK THEOLOGY AND HERMENEUTICS

Blount, Brian. *Can I Get a Witness?: Reading Revelation through African American Culture*. Louisville: Westminster John Knox Press, 2005.

_____. *Cultural Interpretation: Reorienting New Testament Criticism*. Minneapolis: Fortress Press, 1995.

Cone, James H. *Black Theology and Black Power*. New York: Seabury Press, 1969.

_____. *A Black Theology of Liberation*. Maryknoll, NY: Orbis Books, 1990.

_____. "Calling the Oppressors to Account for Four Centuries of Terror." In *Currents in Theology and Mission* 31:3 (June 2004): 179–186.

_____. *For My People: Black Theology and the Black Church*. Maryknoll, NY: Orbis Books, 1984.

_____. *God of the Oppressed*. San Francisco: Harper San Francisco, 1975; Maryknoll, NY: Orbis Books, 1997.

_____. "Looking Back, Going Forward: Black Theology as Public Theology." In *Black Faith and Public Talk: Critical Essays on James H. Cone's Black Theology and Black Power*, ed. Dwight N. Hopkins. Maryknoll, NY: Orbis Books, 1999, 246–260.

_____. *Martin & Malcolm & America: A Dream or a Nightmare*. Maryknoll, NY: Orbis Books, 1991.

_____. *My Soul Looks Back*. Maryknoll, NY: Orbis Books, 1986.

_____. *Risks of Faith: The Emergence of a Black Theology of Liberation, 1968–1998*. Boston: Beacon Press, 1999.

_____. *Speaking the Truth: Ecumenism, Liberation, and Black Theology*. Grand Rapids, MI: Eerdmans, 1986.

_____. *The Spirituals and the Blues: An Interpretation*. New York: Seabury Press, 1972.

_____. "The White Church and Black Power." In *Black Theology: A Documentary History, Volume I: 1966–1979*, ed. James H. Cone and Gayraud S. Wilmore. Maryknoll, NY: Orbis Books, 1979, 112–132.

_____. "Womanist Theology: Introduction." In *Black Theology: A Documentary History, Volume II: 1980–1992*, 2nd ed., ed. James H. Cone and Gayraud S. Wilmore. Maryknoll, NY: Orbis Books, 1993, 257–264.

Cone, James H. and Gayraud S. Wilmore, eds. *Black Theology: A Documentary History, Volume I: 1966–1979*. Maryknoll, NY: Orbis Books, 1979.

Cone, James H. and Gayraud S. Wilmore, eds. *Black Theology: A Documentary History, Volume II: 1980–1992*, 2nd ed. Maryknoll, NY: Orbis Books, 1993.

Davis, Reginald F. "African-American Interpretation of Scripture." *The Journal of Religious Thought*, 57–58:2–2 (2001–2005), 93–105.

Douglas, Kelly Brown. *The Black Christ*. Maryknoll, NY: Orbis Books, 1994.

Evans, James H., Jr. *We Have Been Believers: An African-American Systematic Theology.* Minneapolis: Fortress Press, 1992.

Felder, Cain Hope, ed. *Stony the Road We Trod: African American Biblical Interpretation.* Minneapolis: Fortress Press, 1991.

———. *Troubling Biblical Waters: Race, Class, and Family.* Maryknoll, NY: Orbis Books, 1989.

Grant, Jacquelyn. "Womanist Jesus and the Mutual Struggle for Liberation and on Containing God (Matthew 17:1–7 with Special Emphasis on Matthew 17:4)." *Journal of the Interdenominational Theological Center* 31:1–2 (Fall-Spring 2003–2004): 3–33.

Hopkins, Dwight N. *Being Human: Race, Culture, and Religion.* Minneapolis: Fortress Press, 2004.

———, ed. *Black Faith and Public Talk: Critical Essays on James H. Cone's Black Theology and Black Power.* Maryknoll, NY: Orbis Books, 1999.

———. *Down, Up, and Over: Slave Religion and Black Theology.* Minneapolis: Fortress Press, 2000.

———. *Heart and Head: Black Theology Past, Present, and Future.* New York: Palgrave, 2002.

Paris, Peter J. *The Social Teachings of the Black Churches.* Philadelphia: Fortress Press, 1985.

Pinn, Anthony B. *Terror and Triumph: The Nature of Black Religion.* Minneapolis: Fortress Press, 2003.

Roberts, J. Deotis. *A Black Political Theology.* Philadelphia: Westminster Press, 1974.

———. *Black Religion, Black Theology: The Collected Essays of J. Deotis Roberts.* Harrisburg, PA: Trinity Press International, 2003.

———. *Black Theology in Dialogue.* Philadelphia: Westminster Press, 1987.

———. *Liberation and Reconciliation,* 2nd ed. Louisville: Westminster John Knox Press, 2005.

Sanders, Cheryl J. *Empowerment Ethics for a Liberated People: A Path to African American Social Transformation.* Minneapolis: Fortress Press, 1995.

West, Cornel. *Prophesy Deliverance!: An Afro-American Revolutionary Christianity.* Philadelphia: Westminster Press, 1982.

Williams, Delores S. *Sisters in the Wilderness,* 2nd ed. Maryknoll, NY: Orbis Books, 1995.

EVALUATIONS OF BLACK THEOLOGY AND CULTURE

Carter, Anthony. *On Being Black and Reformed: A New Perspective on the African-American Christian Experience.* Phillipsburg, NJ: P&R, 2003.

Ellis, Carl, Jr. *Free At Last?: The Gospel in the African-American Experience.* Downers Grove, IL: InterVarsity Press, 1996.

———. *Going Global: The Role of the Black Church in the Great Commission of Jesus Christ.* Chicago: Urban Ministries, 2005.

Fields, Bruce. *Introducing Black Theology: Three Crucial Questions for the Evangelical Church.* Grand Rapids, MI: Baker Academic, 2001.

Kee, Alistair. *The Rise and Demise of Black Theology*. Aldershot, UK: Ashgate Publishing Limited, 2006.

Sowell, Thomas. *A Conflict of Visions*. New York: W. Morrow, 1987.

_____. *Barbarians Inside the Gates: And Other Controversial Essays*. Stanford, CA: Hoover Institution Press, 1999.

_____. *Basic Economics: A Citizen's Guide to the Economy*. New York: Basic Books, 2003.

_____. *Ethnic America*. New York: Basic Books, 1981.

_____. *Is Reality Optional?: And Other Essays*. Stanford, CA: Hoover Institution Press, 1993.

_____. *Knowledge and Decisions*. New York: Basic Books, 1986.

_____. *Markets and Minorities*. New York: Basic Books, 1981.

_____. *Marxism: Philosophy and Economics*. New York: Quill, 1985.

_____. *Migrations and Cultures: A World View*. New York: Basic Books, 1996.

_____. *Preferential Policies: An International Perspective*. New York: W. Morrow, 1990.

_____. *Race and Culture: A World View*. New York: Basic Books, 1994.

_____. *Race and Economics*. New York: D. McKay, 1975.

_____. *The Quest for Cosmic Justice*. New York: Free Press, 1999.

EVANGELICAL SOURCES

Bahnsen, Greg L. *Van Til's Apologetic: Readings and Analysis*. Phillipsburg, NJ: P&R, 1998.

Bavinck, Herman. *Reformed Dogmatics, Volume 1: Prolegomena*, trans. John Vriend, ed. John Bolt. Grand Rapids, MI: Baker Academic, 2003.

_____. *Reformed Dogmatics, Volume 3: Sin and Salvation*, trans. John Vriend, ed. John Bolt. Grand Rapids, MI: Baker Academic, 2006.

Beisner, E. Calvin. "Justice and Poverty: Two Views Contrasted." In *Christianity and Economics in the Post-Cold War Era: The Oxford Declaration and Beyond*, ed. Herbert Schlossberg, Vinay Samuel, and Ronald Sider, 57–80. Grand Rapids, MI: Eerdmans, 1994.

Berkhof, Louis. *A Summary of Christian Doctrine*. Grand Rapids, MI: Eerdmans, 1934.

_____. *Systematic Theology*. Grand Rapids, MI: Eerdmans, 1993.

Buswell, James O., III. *Slavery Segregation and Scripture*. Grand Rapids, MI: Eerdmans, 1964.

Calvin, John. *Institutes of the Christian Religion*, trans. Henry Beveridge. Grand Rapids, MI: Eerdmans, 1997.

Conn, Harvie M. *Eternal Word and Changing Worlds: Theology, Anthropology, and Mission in Trialogue*. Grand Rapids, MI: Zondervan, 1984.

Cooper-Lewter, Nicholas and Henry H. Mitchell. *Soul Theology: The Heart of American Black Culture*. Nashville: Abingdon Press, 1991.

Doriani, Daniel M. *Getting the Message: A Plan for Interpreting and Applying the Bible*. Phillipsburg, NJ: P&R, 1996.

_____. *Putting the Truth to Work: The Theory and Practice of Biblical Application*. Phillipsburg, NJ: P&R, 2001.

Jones, David Clyde. *Biblical Christian Ethics*. Grand Rapids, MI: Baker Books, 1994.

Kuyper, Abraham. *Lectures on Calvinism*. Grand Rapids, MI: Eerdmans, 1994.

_____. *The Problem of Poverty*, ed. James W. Skillen. Grand Rapids, MI: Baker Books, 1991.

Poythress, Vern. "Science and Hermeneutics." In *Foundations of Contemporary Interpretation*, ed. Moises Silva, 430–531. Grand Rapids, MI: Zondervan, 1996.

Silva, Moises. "Has the Church Misread the Bible?" In *Foundations of Contemporary Interpretation*, ed. Moises Silva, 11–90. Grand Rapids, MI: Zondervan, 1996.

Van Groningen, Gerard. *From Creation to Consummation*. Sioux Center, IA: Dordt College Press, 1997.

Vanhoozer, Kevin. *The Drama of Doctrine: A Canonical-Linguistic Approach to Christian Theology*. Louisville: Westminster John Knox Press, 2005.

_____. *Is There a Meaning in This Text?: The Bible, the Reader, and the Morality of Literary Knowledge*. Grand Rapids, MI: Zondervan, 1998.

Wright, Christopher J. H. *The Mission of God: Unlocking the Bible's Grand Narrative*. Downers Grove, IL: InterVarsity Press, 2006.

Scripture Index

General Index